Time and History: A Study on the Revelation

TIME
AND HISTORY
A Study on the Revelation

MATHIAS RISSI

translated by Gordon C. Winsor

". . . what is and what is to take place hereafter. . . ."

JOHN KNOX PRESS
Richmond, Virginia

A translation of *Was ist und was geschehen soll danach,* published by Zwingli-Verlag, Zürich, 1965.

Citations of the Old and New Testaments and the Apocrypha refer to the Holy Bible (1946, 1952) and the Apocrypha (1957), Revised Standard Version.

LIBRARY OF CONGRESS CATALOG CARD NUMBER: 66-11904
© M. E. BRATCHER 1966
PRINTED IN THE UNITED STATES OF AMERICA
J.3120

EDUARD THURNEYSEN
in deepest gratitude

FOREWORD

All the books of the New Testament are concerned with history, for God's revelation is disclosed to us in history and has created history. Christian theology has therefore been forced in every age to involve itself with the problematic nature of history. This problem has come to our age with special intensity, for in our time the pressing question of the nature of history is being put anew.[1]

But in no other book of the New Testament has history become so centrally the proper object of theological discussion as it has in the Revelation to John. The intention of this book is not simply to devise a general theology of history, but to lay out, quite concretely, a prophetic interpretation of that history which lies between those two divine interventions which are so very decisive for all human history, between the historically datable first appearance of Jesus Christ and his return.

The present study confines itself to a historical investigation into the basic structure of the understanding of history to be found in the Johannine Revelation and seeks to show how fundamental this understanding is for the exposition of the book as a whole.

---

1 See O. Cullmann, *Christ and Time*, rev. ed. (1962); K. Löwith, *Meaning in History* (1949); A. J. Toynbee, *A Study of History* (1934-1939); K. Barth, *Church Dogmatics;* R. Bultmann, *History and Eschatology* (1958); W. Pannenberg, *Offenbarung als Geschichte* (1961); W. Kreck, *Die Zukunft des Gekommenen* (1961).

ABBREVIATIONS

Apk. and Joh. Apk.	The Revelation to John
AT or OT	The Old Testament
ATANT	*Abhandlungen zur Theologie des Alten und Neuen Testaments,* ed. W. Eichrodt and O. Cullmann
BFTh	*Beiträge zur Förderung christlicher Theologie*
BZ	*Biblische Zeitschrift*
ETL	*Ephemerides Theologicae Lovanienses*
Ev. Theol.	*Evangelische Theologie*
FGK	*Forschungen zur Geschichte des neutestamentlichen Kanons und der altchristlichen Literatur*
FRL	*Forschungen zur Religion und Literatur des Alten und Neuen Testaments*
Hdb. L.	*Handbuch zum Neuen Testament,* founded by H. Lietzmann, ed. G. Bornkamm
ICC	*International Critical Commentary*
JBL	*Journal of Biblical Literature*
NT	The New Testament
NTD	*Das Neue Testament Deutsch, Neues Göttinger Bibelwerk*
NTS	*New Testament Studies*
RB	*Revue biblique*
RGG	*Die Religion in Geschichte und Gegenwart,* ed. K. Galling, 3rd ed. (1957ff.)
RHPR	*Revue d'histoire et de philosophie religieuses*
Riv. Bibl.	*Rivista Biblica*
ThBl	*Theologische Blätter*
Theol. Stud.	*Theologische Studien*

Theol. Stud. u. Krit.	*Theologische Studien und Kritiken*
ThLZ	*Theologische Literaturzeitung*
ThR	*Theologische Rundschau*
ThZ	*Theologische Zeitschrift der theologischen Fakultät der Universität Basel*
TS	*Theological Studies*
TU	*Texte und Untersuchungen zur Geschichte der altchristlichen Literatur*
TWB	*Theologisches Wörterbuch zum NT, founded by G. Kittel, ed. G. Friedrich (1932ff.)*
ZAW	*Zeitschrift für die alttestamentliche Wissenschaft*
ZNW	*Zeitschrift für die neutestamentliche Wissenschaft und die Kunde des Urchristentums*

Contents

I

The Structure
of the Revelation to John

1.

In scarcely any other biblical book are the method of exposition
and the understanding of the book's literary structure so thoroughly
intertwined as they are in the Revelation to John. The question
of construction deeply touches the highly problematic character
of the book. The organization of the total work itself discloses a
distinctive theological interpretation of history.[1]

I hold that it is methodologically improper first of all to tear a
section of the Revelation out of its context, to examine it according to some particular method, and then, if it halfway yields the
desired answer, to regard the correctness of the method for the
investigation of the whole book as proved.[2]

We intend therefore to deal first with the range of the whole
book and to use as a beginning point a difficulty with which all
expositions must come to grips and which is decisive for a right
understanding of the book as a whole. That is to say, we note
that strewn over the whole book again and again there are found
more or less detailed sketches of the Last Day. Is this perhaps
only an illusion, might the visions of the entire book portray
rather a continuous event? Or do these portrayals of the End
comprise proleptic views of the End, inserted in the book in a

---

1 On the question of method, cf. especially P. Prigent, *Apocalypse 12, Histoire de
l'éxégèse* (1959); O. Piper, "Johannesapokalypse," *RGG* 3, 3rd ed. (1959), pp. 822ff.;
A. Feuillet, *L'Apocalypse, État de la question* (1963).

2 For this reason we should be wary of interpretations in terms of church or world
history, e.g., J. A. Bengel, *Erklärte Offenbarung Johannis* (1740). The interpretation
of S. Giet, *L'Apocalypse et l'Histoire* (1957), in terms of events contemporary to John,
is not free of this error.

strangely inorganic manner? Is there a definite suggestion given here that perhaps the Apocalyptist understands his visions as recapitulations? Is there a glimmering in these places that the process of working from sources was not entirely well done?

We see that it is an unavoidable necessity for our study that we begin by making up our minds about the overall structure of the Revelation. Especially must we become quite clear on the question of whether the portrayals of the End prior to 19:11ff. really carry in themselves all the signs of a representation of the Eschaton. The confirmation of this is a question which must be asked in the further study of the significance of its theology of history.

We shall combine with the study of these problematic passages a brief survey of the contents of the Revelation.

The servant of Jesus Christ, John, has received the contents of the book of God and Christ through the mediation of an angel (1:1-3). He delivers the message to the seven churches in Asia and greets them with an introduction like that of a letter (1:4-8). There follows in 1:9-20 a shining vision of the Son of Man in the midst of the lampstands (congregations). Seven messages are addressed to the congregations by the Seer, which are contained in chapters 2 and 3.

With chapter 4 a new series of revelations begins. John sees God in heaven with his royal court, and the Lamb who alone is worthy to open the sealed book (4–5). The opening of the seven seals of the book occurs in 6:1–8:1. In the sixth seal John openly beholds for the first time the beginning of the End of the world. And with this we stand before the first of the problematic "End scenes."

The meaning of the seventh seal scene is made quite clear by the final verse, 6:17: it speaks of the immediate breaking in of the Day of the Lord promised in the Old Testament. This day will bring judgment[3] and therefore Zephaniah 1:15 calls it a "day of wrath . . . of distress and anguish . . . of darkness and gloom . . . and thick darkness" (cf. Amos 5:18-20). All the details serve in this characterization of the scene. They are all taken from

---

3 Joel 2:11, 31; Malachi 3:2.

the Old Testament and show us the originality of the Revelation in its usage of words and conceptions from that source. No direct citations are given, but Old Testament words and attitudes are taken over and worked in to fresh settings.[4]

Mighty earthquakes, convulsive changes in the stars, give notice of the overthrow and destruction of the cosmos,[5] and the anguish of men is intensified to the extreme.[6] We stand directly before the revelation of the great world judgment.[7] Therefore we expect in the seventh seal a portrayal of the End.

But before this happens, a wholly different scene intervenes, the sealing of the 144,000 servants of God (ch. 7). After the sealing, the four angels are permitted to loose their destructive winds. In the second part of this insertion, John sees before the throne of God in heaven an uncountable multitude who have washed their robes in the blood of the Lamb.

Then, in 8:1, there follows the opening of the seventh seal: "there was silence in heaven for about half an hour." The peculiar shortness of the scene has given rise to various conjectures. A psychologizing understanding of the silence as a mere expression of ecstatic experience is certainly to be excluded.[8] That 8:1 is intended only to mark a transition to the next series of seven trumpet visions is in no way suggested in the text[9] and would

---

4 Cf. A. Schlatter, *Das Alte Testament in der johanneischen Apokalypse*, BFTh 16:6 (1912). E. Lohse, "Die alttestamentliche Sprache des Sehers Johannes," *ZNW* 52 (1961), pp. 122–126. A. Vanhoye, "L'utilisation du livre d'Ézéchiel dans l'Apocalypse," *Biblica* 43 (1962), pp. 436–476.

5 Amos 8:9; Isaiah 13:10, 13; 50:3; Joel 2:2, 10, 31; Isaiah 24:3ff.; 34:4; Ezekiel 32:7f. Cf. W. Bousset and H. Gressmann, *Die Religion des Judentums im späthellenistischen Zeitalter*, Hdb. L., Vol. 21, 3rd ed. (1926), pp. 274f. Similarly, Mark 13:24ff.; cf. Stählin, *TWB* 7:61.

6 Isaiah 2:10–21; Hosea 10:8; Joel 2:11; Zephaniah 1:14–18; Malachi 3:2. Cf. P. Volz, *Die Eschatologie der jüdischen Gemeinde im neutestamentlichen Zeitalter* (1934), pp. 277ff., 335.

7 Bousset also maintains in his commentary that the Apocalyptist here "employs details which are customarily employed in depicting the last great day of judgment" (*Die Offenbarung Johannes, Kritisch-exegetischer Kommentar über das NT*, ed. H. A. W. Meyer, 6th ed. [1906], p. 276), and Jülicher and Fascher, *Einleitung in das NT* (1931), p. 250, justly point out that the shattering events in 6:12ff. are enacted as in the following first trumpet vision. Their assumption, that "the later told, respectively later seen, is always the later fufilled as well," impels them to speak of serious deficiencies of composition. The deficiencies could, however, as easily be laid to the account of the expositors who do violence to the text.

8 Bousset, *Die Religion des Judentums*, p. 395.

9 In any event, there is no basis for Jülicher and Fascher to say, "For the seventh seal . . . there remains no content, if we do not regard the next set of seven as an

scarcely account for the designation of the silence with this odd terminology.[10] And just as the sixth seal has already led directly to the End event, we anticipate in the seventh seal, as the conclusion of the whole series, a presentation of the Eschaton.[11] Thus it is methodologically correct to inquire next whether there lie, in the scope of the Seer's spiritual home, eschatological conceptions which could account for the silence in this sense. In fact, we do find in Judaism a clear conception of the eschatological silence.

The "silence" belongs to the creation myth in 2 Esdras 6:39: at the creation there was total stillness, "then the Spirit was hovering, and darkness and silence embraced everything; the sound of man's voice was not yet there." Syriac Baruch 3:7 laments over the impending destruction of Jerusalem: ". . . shall the universe return to its [primeval] nature? And shall the world again lapse into the silence which existed originally?" Pseudo-Philo 60:2, in the psalm which David sings before the dejected Saul, speaks similarly: "Before the world came to be, was darkness and silence."

According to the apocalyptic rule that the primeval time would be a prototype of the End time, it is expected from a part of the Jewish apocalyptic that the world will again sink back into primeval silence and a new world will arise out of the chaos.[12] Thus 2 Esdras 7:29ff.: after the revealing of the Messiah for four hundred years, all "who draw human breath" die, even the Messiah himself, and "the world shall be turned back to primeval silence for seven days, as it was at the first beginnings; so that no one shall be

---

expansion of this material" (*op. cit.*, p. 252). J. Weiss (*Die Offenbarung des Johannes, Die Schriften des NT*, ed. J. Weiss, 2nd ed. [1908], *ad loc.*) is quite right when he finds this continuation of 8:1 somewhat "inorganic." One certainly does not perceive "wherefore the writer should have allowed yet one more complete series of plagues to develop out of the seventh seal, through which the progress of the prophecy will not be substantially advanced," Bousset, *Die Offenbarung Johannes*, p. 144. On the whole, it must be positively maintained that the text nowhere intimates that the various vision series evolve out of the previous ones.

10 One could readily think of Chag. 12b, with E. Lohmeyer, *Die Offenbarung des Johannes, Hdb. L.*, Vol. 16, 2nd ed. (1953), p. 73. Boll's derivation (*Aus der Offenbarung Johannes. Hellenistische Studien zum antiken Weltbild der Apk* [1914], pp. 25f.) lies too far from the text.

11 E. Lohse, *Die Offenbarung des Johannes, NTD*, Vol. 11 (1960), p. 49, offers good grounds for this.

12 On the connections with Sabbath speculations, cf. especially W. Rordorf, *Der Sonntag, ATANT* (1962), pp. 46ff.

left. And after seven days the world, which is not yet awake, shall be roused, and that which is corruptible shall perish."[13]

It is to be observed now that the vision of the sixth seal already displays the breaking in of the primeval chaos which is suggested with such brevity in the seventh seal. The same motif appears again in concrete detail in Revelation 18:22-24: the voices and sounds which the old world made so loudly and joyfully are plunged into the primeval silence.[14] Then out of the final silence there appears, in 19:11ff., the divine Logos (19:13)—as at the time of creation. It is conceivable that a tradition is visible here which is similar to one we encounter in Wisdom of Solomon 18:14f., where the "word," while "gentle silence enveloped all things, . . . leaped from heaven . . . a stern warrior."[15]

Thus what is seen in 8:1 shows itself to be a suggestive portrayal of the eschatological hope, which is fully developed from 19:11ff. on.

However, the source of the temporal designation *hēmiōros* (which occurs neither in the LXX nor in the New Testament) has not yet been found in any parallels from other religions, nor has its particular meaning here been convincingly shown. Perhaps we may come closer to the solution if we consider the meaning of the concept "hour" in the Revelation. "Hour" can be used to indicate a particular event of salvation history[16] and to serve in special instances as a designation of God's great hour (14:7, 15),[17] which includes both the judgment and the gathering of the elect.[18] Hence it is quite possible to presume that the Apocalyptist, in 8:1, where he speaks only of the sinking of the old world into

---

13 Whether John 9:4, "night comes, when no one can work," speaks likewise of this eschatological-chaotic condition of the world, cannot be determined with certainty. Cf. especially G. Stählin, "Zum Problem der johanneischen Eschatologie," *ZNW* 31 (1934), pp. 244–245; O. Cullmann, "Sabbat und Sonntag nach dem Johannesevangelium" (*in memoriam E. Lohmeyer* [1951]), pp. 127–131; W. Rordorf, *op. cit.,* pp. 97–99.

14 The Jewish tradition of the primeval silence also speaks in a special manner of the human voice: "the sound of man's voice was not yet there" (2 Esd. 6:39).

15 Cf. G. Kuhn, "Beiträge zur Erklärung des Buches der Weisheit," *ZNW* 28 (1929), pp. 334–341; and G. Bertram, "Praeparatio evangelica in der Septuaginta," *Vetus Testamentum* 7 (1957), pp. 225–249, sees a connection between Wisdom of Solomon 18:14ff., with its LXX translation of *dbr* as "plague," and the *logos* of Revelation 19:11ff. (pp. 239f.). Cf. Ignatius to the Magnesians 8:2: God's Logos is *apo sigēs proelthōn*.

16 Cf. p. 29 of this book.

17 See the previous footnote. Mark 13:32 speaks similarly of the eschatological hour which no one knows but the Father.

18 See below.

primeval silence, had used *hēmiōros* to indicate the first, dark half of God's great eschatological hour, which the other half, the bright new creation, will then follow. Only then is the whole hour of God brought to its fulfillment.

A new vision begins in 8:2 with an introduction (8:2-6). The angels who stand before God receive seven trumpets; meanwhile, another angel with a golden censer brings incense to the altar for the prayers of the saints. He swings the censer to the earth as a prelude to a long series of visions which will be ushered in through the blast of the trumpets. Just as the previous seal visions were divided into a 4 + 3 arrangement (through the same pictorial element of four horsemen), so here the trumpets are similarly employed, while the latter three are introduced through an eagle as the three "woes" (8:13).

The fifth trumpet with its plague constitutes the first woe (9:12); the two further woes are announced. The second woe can refer only to the sixth trumpet vision. The fact that the Seer does not speak of the completion of the second woe before 11:14, after the presentation of the two scenes inserted between the sixth and seventh visions, does not contradict *this,* for with a formula similar to 9:12 the confirmation of the realization of the plague is tied to the announcement of the arrival of the last woe. Thus the natural place of the formula is directly before the blast of the seventh trumpet, which announces the coming of the judgment (11:18).

The first six trumpet visions appear to go back to traditional motifs which are also recognizable in the Egyptian plagues of the Old Testament, although formed with great independence.[19]

Again the sixth scene is given special emphasis in the series. "With the sixth trumpet a fearful scene discloses itself, to which the preceding scenes are related only as a prelude."[20] This scene leads (as does the sixth seal) further to the final intensifying and extending of the apocalyptic events.[21] The special significance of

---

19 Cf. the commentaries and now especially H. P. Müller, "Die Plagen der Apokalypse, Eine formgeschichtliche Untersuchung," *ZNW* 51 (1960), pp. 268–278.

20 E. Lohse, *Die Offenbarung des Johannes, NTD,* p. 54.

21 Note the far-reaching group of four angels, the monstrous horde of horses and riders. That it concerns the battle of the Antichrist with Christendom (Th. Zahn, *Die*

the plague is stressed by its reference to the altar which stands before God (9:13), by the direct command which summons from the altar the execution of a plague whose timing is fixed with complete precision (9:15).

Between the sixth and seventh trumpets there is again inserted a two-part interlude (10–11): a mighty angel with a face shining like the sun announces the speedy End of the temporal world, which will begin with the seventh trumpet (10:7). During this scene John hears seven thunders, whose words are however not intended to be passed on to the churches (10:4). A heavenly voice orders John to eat the scroll which the mighty angel holds and once more to prophesy.

The second part of the interlude should probably be understood as the content of the scroll. John must measure a part of the temple which is to be given over to trampling by the nations (11:1-2). During the forty-two months (or 1,260 days) two witnesses appear in the city, who are killed at the end of their time by the beast from the bottomless pit. Their dead bodies lie desecrated in the street of the city three and one-half days while all the peoples rejoice. But then they rise up living again and go up to heaven. In a mighty earthquake, which produces terror before God in a part of the inhabitants, the city is smashed.

The third woe (seventh trumpet) again leads on to God's eschatological day. In two hymns, full of allusions to Old Testament expressions, the celebration of the entrance of the End (already announced in 10:7) is the chief point. The royal authority of God and of Christ is now evident. Psalm 2 has found its final fulfillment. God has answered the wrath of the peoples with his own wrath (Rev. 11:18a; Ps. 2:1, 5) and his judgment on the living and the dead. Because it is the final future that is involved here, God is called here only "who art and who wast" (cf. 1:8). "God is no longer coming, he is now there."[22] At the same time,

---

Offenbarung Johannes, Kommentar zum NT, ed. Th. Zahn, Vol. 18 [1924–1926], pp. 403–408), is nowhere indicated in the text; indeed, it is excluded by 9:20.

22 E. Lohmeyer, *op. cit., ad loc.* Only a violent reinterpretation of the text can see here an intermezzo "with proleptic meaning" (so Bousset, *op. cit., ad loc.*) or "the shell" for the following visions (Lohmeyer, *loc. cit.*).

the End is the occasion for jubilation by the redeemed, for the royal lordship now lies indisputably in God's hands.

The two hymns are followed by the opening of the heavenly temple, which emphasizes the event-like character of the seventh trumpet and allows the End event to appear in its consummation.[23] The Holy of Holies of the heavenly temple is opened (cf. 19:11), so that the sign of God's covenant of the Old Testament becomes visible.[24] One ought not lose sight of the very special attachment of the Ark of the Covenant to the people of Israel, whose fate constitutes the content of the immediately preceding section (11:1-13). The End will reveal the faithfulness of God to Israel; the coming salvation of Israel will no longer stand in the sign of the earthly temple and the earthly Ark of the Covenant but will disclose a reality coming from heaven.[25]

Just as the hymns celebrate not only the breaking in of the kingdom but also the coming of the judgment, so also there enters here, adjacent to the sign of salvation, the sign of judgment: lightning, loud noises, thunder, an earthquake, and heavy hail.[26]

In chapter 12, a new series of visions begins: the great sign of the woman who gives birth to the boy. Both are menaced by the dragon. But God snatches away the child and the dragon is cast out of heaven by Michael and his angels. The dragon begins a war with the woman, who, however, remains protected by God during three and one-half times in the desert. The persecution now directs itself against the other children of the woman. In 12:10-12, the scene is interrupted by mighty praise of Christ's victory.

In chapter 13, two beasts appear, endowed with full power by

23 The efforts to separate 11:19 and attach it to chapter 12 are all impossible (E. B. Allo, *Saint Jean, L'Apocalypse* [1921], *ad loc.*). It should not be overlooked that neither in form nor content is verse 19 out of context and that in 12:1 a new vision is introduced. This is properly emphasized by A. Feuillet, "Essai d'interprétation du chapitre 11 de l'Apocalypse," *NTS* 4 (1958), pp. 198f.; cf. L. Cerfaux and J. Cambier, *L'Apocalypse de Saint Jean* (1955), pp. 97–99.

24 On this conception, cf. 2 Maccabees 2:4–8; Apocalypse of Baruch 6:5–10; b. Talmud Horayoth 12a; Josephus, *Ant.* 18:85–87.

25 P. M. É. Boismard rightly emphasizes the opposition to the earthly temple seen here, "L'Apocalypse ou les Apocalypses de Saint Jean," *RB* 56 (1949), p. 511.

26 The special character of God's revelation incorporates grace and salvation at the same time; cf. K. L. Schmidt, "Die Bildersprache in der Johannesapokalypse," *ThZ* 3 (1947), pp. 170f.

the dragon. These take up the persecution and corruption of the saints.

14:1-5 displays the Lamb on Zion accompanied by the one hundred and forty-four thousand. Then an angel, together with a second one, proclaims the end of Babylon and gives warning prior to the judgment. They use this warning to point to the next portrayal of the End of the world in 14:14-20.

The final judgment is set forth in a twofold harvest scene. The first (14:14-16) is a Parousia scene, shaped in a traditional fashion and ultimately based on Daniel 7:13.[27] The objection that the one coming to the judgment is seen sitting on the cloud without any mention of his coming is quite insufficient to establish that in 14:14f. the Parousia of the Messiah is not portrayed,[28] for even in the Parousia scene in 19:11ff. it is not the "coming" that is spoken of but the Messiah's sitting on the white horse.

Because John sees the judgment as a harvest, he ties to the Son of Man portrayal the eschatological harvest-judgment scene of Joel 3:13: "Put in the sickle, for the harvest is ripe."

It has always seemed quite strange that an angel should transmit to Christ the command of God to begin the harvest. But this is not really so astonishing when we observe that this angel is one who comes from the heavenly temple, the dwelling place of God,[29] and that we also encounter in Mark 13:32 the idea that only the Father, not the Son, knows "the hour" of the End.

In order to appreciate fully the special meaning of this harvest scene, one should observe that the saying about the harvest in Joel 3:13 is divided into two distinct scenes. This key statement speaks of both wheat and grape harvests in referring to the judgment on the nations:

---

27 Cf. 1:7. Even Bousset, who seeks to take into account the thinking of "the Apocalyptist's later hand," but who prefers to find in the portrayal of the Son of Man an angel, writes: "There can be no doubt that, according to the original sense of the passage, the figure should be the Messiah." Lohmeyer maintains the identity of the figure in 14:14 with the Messiah. However, he believes that here a variation in the "total eschatological outlook" has entered; that here this figure (contrary to its central value to the synoptists) is used only "as an item in a larger outlook." *Allos* refers to the other angelic figures, not to the Son of Man, who stands out as king (indicated by the golden crown) in the midst of the three announcing and three fulfilling angels in this group of seven.

28 So for instance, T. Holtz, *Die Christologie der Apokalypse des Johannes* (1962), p. 130.

29 Cf. the conception of the "angel of the Lord," G. von Rad, *TWB* 1:75f.

a. "Put in the sickle, for the harvest is ripe."
b. "Go in, tread, for the wine press is full. The vats overflow, for their wickedness is great."

The seeing of the grape harvest as an expression of bloody judgment is utilized in 14:17-20 (cf. Isa. 63:1-6). This punitive judgment is carried out by angels.

It is interesting to note that in the first part of the harvest scene, accomplished by the Son of Man himself, nothing is said about God's wrath. It is highly possible that we are dealing here with the influence of the primitive Christian understanding of the harvest as a symbol for the eschatological gathering of the elect from out of the whole world (Matt. 3:12; 9:37; 13:30; Mark 4:29; 13:27).[30] This tradition is certainly tied to the emphasis put on the eschatological period in Revelation 14:15: "for the hour to reap has come."[31]

The distinction between the two scenes is also attested by the special association of the second scene at the altar. The angel who brings the command for the grape harvest comes forth from the altar (14:18), where according to 6:10, the martyrs await the revelation of the divine justice.[32] The second scene is thus God's answer to the cry of the martyrs. Hence the group of visions in 12–14 also closes with a scene depicting the End.

In chapter 15 a new series of seven scenes begins (with an introduction, 15:1-4). Those who had conquered the beast stand beside the sea of glass and sing the song of Moses and the song of the Lamb. Hereafter begin the seven final plagues, introduced by the angels pouring out on the earth the seven bowls of wrath. They are strikingly like the trumpet visions.

It has often occurred to commentators that 16:15 could scarcely have stood originally in its present place, for the verse breaks into the portrayal of the sixth bowl scene very abruptly.[33] No doubt at

---

30 T. Holtz, *op. cit.*, p. 134, properly draws attention to the fact that the Son of Man scene in 1:12ff. also characterizes Christ as the Lord of the churches.

31 Matthew 13:48, *eplērōthē*. See J. Jeremias, *The Parables of Jesus*, 2nd ed. (1963), pp. 151f., 226.

32 Here also is found the problem of the eschatological period, in 6:11!

33 E. Lohmeyer, *op. cit., ad loc.*: "By its form and content the verse is impossible in this place." But to transfer it to a place between 3:3 and 3:4 is completely arbitrary, although suggested by Lohmeyer and Cl. Könnecke, *Emendationen zu Stellen des Neuen Testaments*, BFTh (1908), pp. 34f.; R. H. Charles, *A Critical and Exegetical Commentary on the Revelation of St. John, ICC* (1920), *ad loc.*

a very early time the verse was erroneously transcribed into this place before verse 16. Placed after verse 16 it can be understood without difficulty within the formal order of the apocalyptic seven series simply as a brief interlude between the sixth and seventh bowl visions. The verse thus constitutes a parallel to the interludes in chapter 7 and 10–11. That this interlude is very short is to be explained by the special intention of the formation of the final visions: the rapidity of the conclusion of the events becomes more intense as the End draws near. The final event will be delayed only by the smallest of interludes.

The destruction of the world is again designated in dependence on Old Testament conceptions. The voice coming forth from the throne of God attests again—as in 14:15—to the realization of the eschatological period (16:17). The bowl judgments are carried out, and in them, according to 15:1, God's wrath comes to consummation, therefore *gegonen* points to the end of all judgments within world history. The violence of the earthquake and the hail plague is a sign of the last judgment. Babylon, the center of the powers at enmity with God on earth, is finally broken into three parts, and with it all the cities of the nations fall. In 16:20, the idea of the destruction of the world comes completely into view.[34] In contrast with the people of Jerusalem (11:13), Babylon's inhabitants curse God during the judgment.

With chapter 17 a new section begins, which, through the mention of the angel in 17:1, is brought into particularly close connection with the bowl plagues. Chapter 17 brings a great, drawn-out picture of Babylon and its beast; chapter 18 follows with a final portrayal of Babylon's destruction.

This scene leads on to the hymns of 19:1-10, which, like 11:15-19, celebrate the coming of the kingdom of God. Again, this is pointed on the one hand toward the last judgment within world history (19:2-4), on the other hand to the presently beginning

---

34 Cf. Lohmeyer, *op. cit., ad loc.;* Assumption of Moses 10:4; Enoch 1:6; Sibylline Oracles 7:234ff.; 3:776f. Ezekiel 26:18 is the central emphasis here. In Zahn, *op. cit., ad loc.,* it becomes especially clear how much one must be careful not to alter the text of a passage outrageously, simply to accommodate the general viewpoint. Zahn interprets the reading *pasa nēsos* as "various islands and mountains." Here, however, the reference is to the whole of the world.

blessedness of God's servants (19:5ff.). This blessedness will be especially celebrated in song in the scene of the eschatological marriage of the Lamb. Thus this series of visions is also associated with a view of the End. To this there is attached an exhortation.

With 19:11ff., there begins the last major section of the book, introduced by the Parousia of Christ. The great majority of exegetes properly hold to this interpretation of 19:11-21.[35] Christ comes forth from heaven as the judge of the world.[36] His diadems show his coming as an eschatological king. The following destruction (19:17-21) bears so clearly the character of finality and the proportions of history's end (the Antichrist is absent from this point on) that it is impossible that it can be only a symbol of all Christ's judgments on world history, which "have been always, since the Incarnation, exercised in a manner more or less visible" (Allo, *op. cit., ad loc.*).

Two details in this majestic scene are difficult to understand. They involve the statement that the rider's robe has been dipped in blood and that Christ bears, besides his known name "the Word of God," yet another, unknown name, "which no one knows but himself" (19:12).

The characterization of Christ as the executor of judgment in verse 15 could point to the one who treads the wine press in Isaiah 63:1-3, whose garments are sprinkled with the blood of the nations. But this scene is not simply adopted here; rather, the function of the victor over his enemies is suggested only by the bringing together of two Old Testament reminiscences (Ps. 2:9, which is also used in the word of eschatological judgment in Rev. 11:18, and Joel 3:13, cf. Rev. 14:7-15). Remarkably, there is no mention of a blood-soaked robe in connection with these Old Testament sayings. Therefore it is well to note that Christ already wears the red robe in heaven, before the beginning of the act of judgment. It is much more likely that the Johannine conception of the blood of the Lamb is behind the verse (7:14; 22:14; 1 John 1:7; 5:6) and

---

35 This interpretation has been opposed, not so much on grounds lying within the text itself, but derived from a particular overall understanding of the book. Cf. Allo, who would like to see in the millennium the church in its present state.

36 Cf. Volz, *op. cit.,* pp. 212–214; and *ThZ* (1965), pp. 81ff.

that we should recognize in the blood-soaked robe of the returning Word of God a sign of his forgiving grace.[37]

The "unknown name," which only Christ himself knows,[38] also appears to correspond to a Johannine conception. Even the victors, to whom salvation is promised, will receive a new name, "which no one knows except him who receives it" (2:17). Just as the nature of the person is revealed in his name,[39] even so will the Parousia of Christ bring the unveiling of the true nature, as yet hidden from the world, of Christ as well as of the faithful. First John has a similar expression: "Beloved, we are God's children now; it does not yet appear what we shall be, but we know that when he appears we shall be like him, for we shall see him as he is" (3:2).[40]

The Parousia follows the victory of Christ over his enemies, the beast and the pseudoprophets with their hosts. Before it comes to a real battle, the power of the enemies is broken. 19:17-21 is more an act of judgment than a combat.

With 20:1ff., there follows the binding of Satan for a thousand years, during which time Christ rules with his own (after their resurrection). Thereafter the Satan will be freed one more time. He deceives the peoples at the four corners of the earth. Gog and Magog march against the beloved city, but are overwhelmed by a fiery judgment. Satan is thrown into the lake of fire (20:7-10).

The final judgment then follows, the destruction of the whole world (20:11-15), and in 21–22 its new creation. The new Jeru-

---

37 A. Schlatter, *op. cit.*, p. 47, considers Genesis 49:11 to be the basic passage, for, "while *bebammenon* is said of the blood, it may be brought intentionally to the garment (as in Gen. 49:11). Thus John seems to have employed Genesis 49:11 for the church which therefore has access to God, because they washed their garments in the blood of the Lamb (7:14); thus it is questionable whether John has the blood of enemies in mind. In contrast to the tradition, he intends to connect the verse with the memory of Jesus' cross. Through this the blood becomes the adornment of Christ, while the Lamb stands slaughtered before God."

38 The fact that only Christ himself knows the name makes it impossible to think that the names mentioned in 19:11, 13, 16, are in mind here. Neither the meaning "Yahweh" (a possibility according to Hadorn), nor an allusion to a name used for conjuring (Bousset, *op. cit., ad loc.*), will square with the text and bring any kind of clarification, nor yet the thought that here only the inscription of the name might be meant and *oudeis* include only the worshipers of the beast (Lohmeyer, *op. cit., ad loc.*).

39 Cf. Bousset, *Die Religion des Judentums*, p. 263, and H. Bietenhard, *TWB* 5:242ff.

40 Cf. the Jewish outlook, as in Pesiktha 148a: "Six things will God someday restore, and these are: heaven, the earth, the heart, the Spirit, the name of the Messiah, and the name of Jerusalem," H. L. Strack and P. Billerbeck, *Kommentar zum NT aus Talmud und Midrasch* (1922–1928), 3:797.

salem comes from heaven (ch. 21), and the whole world becomes the realm of God's absolute dominion (22:1-5).

The conclusion of the book is composed of the exhortations of Christ (22:6-7), of the angel (22:8-11), then again of Christ (22:12-16), and of John (22:18-21).

2.

In this review of the content of the book as a whole a definite conformity to certain structural principles of the outline becomes recognizable. The text of the Revelation divides itself into three major groups:

1) The message to the seven churches of Asia Minor, 1–3. John speaks first of his commission in the manner of the Old Testament prophets, 1:1-3 (cf. Hos. 1:1, Isa. 1:1; as a Christian, the Seer alters the Old Testament form). He then greets the churches with his salutation, 1:4-8. The call-vision and the letters to the seven churches follow.

2) The vision groups, which all terminate with a portrayal of the End of this aeon and thus evidently include the time until the Parousia (4:1–19:10). The kind and manner of visions, as these scenes of the End follow one after another, display a distinct plan of composition: the scenes become ever richer and more colorful from the mysterious intimations in 8:1 on—that is, the visions of 11:15-19; 14:14-20; 16:17–19:10, and the conclusions of the interludes—until the mighty vision in chapter 19. This midsection of the book divides itself into the three series of seven each, involving the seals, the trumpets, and the bowls. Between the two latter there is intruded a further series of visions which, through its arrangement in the total structure of 4:1–19:10, is obviously to be recognized as a connected unity like the seals, trumpets, and bowls. Also, 12:1–14:20, parallel to the seals, trumpets, and bowls, is concluded by a portrayal of the End event. The whole midsection of our book is thus constructed out of the following groups (beginning with the two great visions of God and the Lamb): 4:1-11; 5:1-14; 6:1–8:1; 8:2–11:19; 12:1–14:20; 15:1–16:21; 17:1–19:10.

3) The visions and sayings, which embrace the development of

the coming of the kingdom of God after the great Parousia scene of 19:11ff. (19:11–22:21). Whether the third part is also arranged in a sevenfold pattern, and whether the formula "then I saw" is to be regarded as a criterion of organization (19:11, 17, 19; 20:1, 4, 11; 21:1), appears questionable to me, for the formula emerges in 20:12 and 21:1 and, so, in 20:7, 21:9, and 22:1 is to be recognized as clearly beginning a new section. Because the *formal* criteria are dubious, one could discover with respect to the *content* of 19:11–20:15 seven single units: Parousia (19:11-16), summons to the eschatological banquet (19:17-18), judgment (19:19-21), binding of Satan (20:1-3), first resurrection in the millennium (20:4-6), victory over Gog and Magog (20:7-10), world judgment (20:11-15). Three final scenes are attached to these: announcement of the new Jerusalem (21:1-8), description of the new Jerusalem (21:9-27), consummated world (22:1-5). It is not surprising that the visions conclude with a group of three, for the number three stands in a special relationship to God; cf. the threefold designation of God (1:4-6; 19:6); the threefold "holy" carries three divine predicates (4:8); threefold acclamation (4:11; cf. 19:1); creation is described with three expressions (4:11); and the great scene showing the adversary as an antitype of God is wholly governed by the number three (ch. 12f.).[41]

Thus the following overall plan of the book may be developed:[42]

I. Message to the seven churches:
    1. Commission, 1:1-3
    2. Greeting, 1:4-8
    3. Call vision, 1:9-20
    4. Messages to the seven churches, 2–3

II. Visions of the End time:
    1. God's throne, 4
    2. The book and the Lamb, 5

41 Cf. A. Farrer, *A Rebirth of Images* (1949), pp. 48f.

42 The number seven as the basic structure of the book has been especially worked out by R. H. Charles, *op. cit.*, E. Lohmeyer, *op. cit.* J. W. Bowman attempts to discover in the Revelation the form of a drama (*The Drama of the Book of Revelation* [1955] and "The Revelation to John: Its Dramatic Structure and Message," *Interpretation* 9 [1955], pp. 436–453; I offer here a different arrangement from the one Bowman cites in his tables from the first edition of my book).

	3. The seven seals, 6:1–8:1
	4. The seven trumpets, 8:2–11:19
	5. The adversary and the Lamb, 12–14
	6. The seven bowls, 15:1–16:21
	7. Babylon, its beast, and their fall, 17:1–19:10
III. The return of Christ:	1. Parousia, 19:11-16
	2. Summons to the eschatological meal, 19:17f.
	3. Downfall of the world powers, 19:19-21
	4. Binding of Satan, 20:1-3
	5. The millennial kingdom, 20:4-6
	6. Fall of Gog and Magog, 20:7-10
	7. World judgment, 20:11-15
IV. The new creation:	1. Praise of the new Jerusalem, 21:1-8
	2. The new Jerusalem, 21:9-27
	3. The new world, 22:1-5
	4. Epilogue, 22:6-21

A formal particularity which is significant for the understanding of the book as a whole yet remains to be mentioned. We have seen that in the vision series of the second major section, those conceived in groups of seven, an interlude intrudes itself between the sixth and seventh scenes. In both chapters 7 and 11 this interlude is in the form of a double scene, while in chapter 16 it forms a double saying.

So far, the formal configuration of the book is clearly recognizable. There is a further question, which yields inferences for the clarification of the book's content, above all for its comprehension of history. This question will have to be investigated more precisely in the course of the study.

3.

It will not be wholly unimportant to add here a further word concerning the artistry of the Seer as it shows itself in the structuring of his work. Opinions diverge greatly concerning this. Very often the outline of the book is called "ingenious," the Revelation a "learned" work, composed in a scholar's study.[43] Ernst Lohmeyer however has conclusively shown with fine artistic discernment that in the Revelation a work of authentic art lies before us, fashioned with great creative power.[44] Recent study has largely moved on from the many attempts at dissection based on literary criticism because of considerations of linguistics, form, and content in the Revelation.[45] So long as the composition lying before us is complete and clearly understandable in itself, as is confirmed by our studies, one must be on guard against arbitrarily breaking up the text and reconstructing it according to one's own plan, explaining all not immediately transparent passages as failures of memory on the editor's part or as broken places caused by the putting together of distinct sources and fragments. The proper comprehension of the structural norms of a literary work always naturally remains to a certain degree dependent on the ability of the reader to recognize the structural design of the work and to allow it to have its own effect on him.

We shall seek to show that the Revelation's comprehension of time and history permits the whole book to appear as an integrated

---

43 Jülicher and Fascher, *op. cit.*, p. 247.

44 W. Michaelis, *Einleitung in das Neue Testament,* 2nd ed. (1954), pp. 308f., holds a similar opinion.

45 Recent studies generally assume the linguistic unity of the whole book. P. Gaechter holds that the Revelation was written by a pupil of the Apostle John, whose discourses were written down with the individual parts in a confused order ("Semitic Literary Forms in the Apc. and Their Import," *TS* 8 [1947]; "The Role of Memory in the Making of the Apc.," *TS* 9 [1948]; "The Original Sequence of Apc. 20–22," *TS* 10 [1949]). Boismard, disturbed by the many "doublets," attempts to separate the book into two apocalypses, written by the same author and later brought together (*op. cit.*, pp. 507–541, and in his commentary *L'Apocalypse, La sainte Bible* [1953], pp. 10–12). But their criteria are insufficient. On this, see the excellent discussions of W. Michaelis, *op. cit.,* pp. 306–309, and W. G. Kümmel, *Einleitung in das Neue Testament* (1963), pp. 338f.; O. Piper, *op. cit.*, pp. 826f.

unity which can only derive from the formative will of a single author.[46]

4.

The question of the genuineness of the visions naturally poses a special problem. We cannot consider in this place the whole complex question which enters here; we shall be content with a few suggestions. The answer is not decisive for the outcome of our study.

How is a work of such an artful plan, interwoven with traditional arguments, compatible with the genuine agitation and emotion of a prophet and ecstatic? To this problem I should like to call attention to the work of C. Schneider, which has been rather too bluntly depreciated by Lohmeyer.[47] Schneider has urged several insights which ought not remain unnoticed. Thus he has pointed to the example of the "robe mysticism" to show how certain traditional scenes become, during ecstasy, a part of our own experience, so that they attract to themselves "certain complex qualities of disposition."[48] In this way, it is to be seen as at least a psychological possibility that the visions of the Revelation can have run in the traditional seven series for the reason that the number was especially meaningful for the Seer. On the other hand, it is also to be noted that the Apocalyptist can in all freedom omit the sevenfold arrangement on occasion (12:1–14:20; 17:1–19:10).[49] The question of genuineness in visionary portrayals naturally presents itself in the same manner in other similar literary works (for instance, in the book of Daniel[50] and in the extracanonical Christian apocalypses such as the Shepherd of Hermas). In any event, the answer to this question will always remain a calculation of probabilities for those works whose origins lie so far distant from our time. We can hold to no more than the possibility.

---

46 Naturally, this does not exclude later additions which actualize the book's message. We shall return to this point later.

47 E. Lohmeyer, "Die Offenbarung des Johannes, 1910–1934," *ThR* (1935), pp. 39f.

48 C. Schneider, *Die Erlebnisechtheit der Apokalypse Johannes* (1930), p. 44.

49 The attempts to see even here the sevenfold structures are much too ingenious and violent (cf. Lohmeyer's commentary).

50 See W. Baumgartner, "Ein Vierteljahrhundert Danielforschung," *ThR* (1939), pp. 138f.

Although nothing of decisive importance for the present study will come forth from the study of this matter, nevertheless I should make brief reference to the inadequacy of the grounds on which objections to the genuineness of the visions have frequently been brought forward.

1) Jülicher and Fascher[51] believe that genuine visions could have underlain the writing only if "in a marvelous way the writing of the book had taken place at the same time as the seeing and hearing."[52] Why however should the author not have been able to write the book after the fading away of his ecstatic states, yet under the indelible impression of his experiences? Genuine vision and subsequent formation in words are not mutually exclusive.[53] The artful arrangement of the book is best to be explained thusly: the Seer has with his poetic power combined his essentially connected experiences into a formal unity subsequent to their occurrence.

2) Jülicher and Fascher (p. 247) and Clemen (pp. 34f.)[54] point to a disorder in relation to the change of position of the Seer in the sequence of his visions, which shows that the effect is that of a putting together of sources and fragments. Thanks to C. Schneider, this problem has been emphasized precisely in its significance for the problem of the genuineness of the visions. In hallucination, people can change their standpoint in the new visions without trouble. The question of the location of the scenes cannot provide a certain basis for source-critical hypotheses.

3) Attention has frequently been called to the "unclarity" of certain scenes or pictorial elements (Jülicher and Fascher, p. 248; Clemen, pp. 36ff.). To that may be said: many scenes are only sketched, so that actually for a full understanding of the text an imagination is thus required which will share to a degree in the experience and creativity of the Seer (for example, in chapters 4–5). But there is also to be considered the question of which incredible contents of the so-called unclear scenes a visionary is

---

51 *Op. cit.,* p. 247.
52 See also P. Gaechter, "The Role of Memory," *op. cit.,* p. 422.
53 And for the interpretation of "write" in 14:13 as "let it be written" (Gaechter, *ibid.*), there is not the least basis.
54 C. Clemen, "Die Bildlichkeit der Offenbarung Johannes," *Festgabe für Julius Kaftan* (1920), pp. 25ff.

able to retain in his memory (Schneider, p. 12). And one ought not overlook the fact that the visionary knows intuitively about things he sees which normally he could not recognize. From its visionary character comes the best clue to the question of the external form of the "book" in chapter 5. There the Seer sees, after the loosing of the several seals, what is contained in the book. Whether the book is a codex or a scroll is of no concern. In any event we cannot comprehend why the Apocalyptist was not able to see the events of the book, even though the book remains externally sealed to the seventh seal. Vision images "must be interpreted and evaluated according to other rules than used for the real images of painters and sculptors."[55] The vision scene is shaped, not from the objective distance of a sober observer, but from an intuitive involvement with the object of the vision. Many peculiarities of the presentation explain themselves also out of the Semitic manner of describing persons and objects, concerning itself much more with nature and function than with form.[56] The real clarity of the much-maligned scenes of the Revelation is shown, however, by the book's effect on the history of art.

4) The reappearance of certain pictorial elements in subsequent visions or the presentation of the same material in various scenes (Jülicher and Fascher, p. 248) does not speak against the genuineness of a vision (cf. Schneider, pp. 13, 19, and other places).

5) It is obvious that there can be no certain distinction made between what has been seen by the author and what is his recreative, poetic transcription of the events. It should be considered that many things became clear to the Seer himself only during his subsequent reflection.[57]

6) That the Revelation usually depicts visionary events in the same manner as the Old Testament and Jewish authors[58] does not signify that this stereotyped manner of expression has simply replaced a genuine vision experience with a literary fiction; rather,

---

55 Against Zahn, *op. cit.*, p. 337. Cf. also the good and cautious opinion in Bousset, *Die Offenbarung Johannes*, pp. 13ff.

56 Cf. Th. Boman, *Hebrew Thought Compared with Greek* (1961), pp. 74–122.

57 Schneider pays too little attention to this. I. P. Seierstad has derived many useful suggestions from the prophet Amos ("Erlebnis und Gehorsam beim Propheten Amos," *ZAW* 52 [1934], pp. 22–41).

58 Cf., for instance, Ezekiel 1:28; Daniel 10:7f.; 10:9; Enoch 14:14, 24f.

it points only to the fact that such experiences with the same God produce each time these same psychic reactions and take shape in similar forms.

One criticism must be applied to the whole of Schneider's work. He has too little regard for the actual content which the visions must have had for the Apocalyptist. Not only do dreams of things longed for, etc., stand behind the visions, but also (as in the case of ecstatic experiences of other great personalities) the ingenious religious and ethical ideas of a creative man, or—better said—the power and the illumination of the Holy Spirit.

The acceptance of the genuineness of the visions is much more capable of clarifying the questions and problems of the text and of doing justice to the text than are the many hypotheses about sources, fragments, and revisions.[59]

The place where the various emerging traditions and traditional elements in the Revelation are assimilated, transformed, and newly formed, is not the writing desk of a learned collector, a redactor, or a poet, but in the vision of the Apocalyptist himself, who is acquainted with the formal relationship of his message to the traditions and who is not afraid occasionally to let this relationship have its effect on the literary outcome of his revelational material.

---

59 Michaelis also favors the genuineness of the visions in his *Einleitung,* pp. 308f. Richard Krämer comes to the same conclusion in his very suggestive interpretation of the Revelation, *Die Offenbarung des Johannes in überzeitlicher Deutung* (1929), pp. 16–25. Krämer calls special attention to the uniqueness of the prophetic "being in the Spirit"; however, he passes too hastily over the correspondence of the psychological phenomenon of ecstasy with the psychic condition of the prophet while receiving revelation—as it is described in the biblical text. God can also make use of this consciousness, apart from the will of the ecstatic, in order to go in a very special manner with the man, while he overwhelms his spirit with his revelational scenes. Cf. W. G. Kümmel, *op. cit.,* p. 340.

II

The Understanding of Time

1. TERMS FOR TIME

In order to arrive at a precise clarification of what time and history mean in the Revelation, it will be necessary first to examine the terminology used for time in the book.

The word *kairos* bears a special significance.[1] The usage of the word in 1:3 and 22:10 is pregnant with theological meaning. In these places the *kairos* is understood as near at hand (*eggus*). Corresponding to the Hebrew '*et*,[2] which the LXX oftentimes translates with *kairos*, the Revelation here takes this word to be a point of time marked out by God through a particular revelational action. In both places the word signifies the end of world history and the inbreaking of the kingdom of God.[3] *Eggus* emphasizes the nearness of this moment.[4] The *kairos* is to be understood so unequivocally as temporally future that in no wise can a "vertical" sense in the manner of some mystics be made out of this "horizontal" view, as Reisner attempts to do.[5] The distinct tone of the announcement of the near End grounds itself on the authority of him who reveals this message: Christ, the eschatological Lord of the church himself (1:1).[6]

---

1 Cf. G. Delling, *TWB* 3:460ff.

2 Cf. C. von Orelli, *Die hebräischen Synonyma der Zeit und Ewigkeit, genetisch und sprachvergleichend dargestellt* (1871), pp. 19, 49ff.; G. Delling, *Das Zeitverständnis des NT* (1940), pp. 49ff.; O. Cullmann, *Christ and Time*, I, 1; E. Jenni, "Time," *The Interpreter's Dictionary of the Bible* (1962), 4:643, 645.

3 Cf. Luke 21:8; 1 Peter 1:5; 5:6.

4 Cf. W. G. Kümmel, *Promise and Fulfilment* (1953), pp. 19ff.

5 E. Reisner, *Das Buch mit den sieben Siegeln* (1949), p. 19: "That whereat the prophecy aims . . . is thus always near insofar as we know ourselves to be situated on the threshold of eternity."

6 The temporal-futuristic meaning of the *kairos* in 22:10 comes out with complete clarity. The urgency of the Revelation's proclamation is grounded here on this temporal nearness of the End.

With this characterization as *kairos,* the End event is designated as that occurrence which enters in the course of time and which itself fills out time. This *kairos,* which is itself a temporal event, thus in no wise refers to "the suspension of time."[7]

In 11:18, *ho kairos* is used pregnantly with the same meaning exactly. Here the context gives the meaning as the moment of final judgment.

Kairos (without article) can also lose its original sense and be used for designating a stretch of time, as in 12:12: *oligon kairon echei* (said of the dragon). Perhaps there is here a basic agreement with the original meaning, in the sense that this time has been determined by God (cf. 1 Cor. 7:5 and Acts 17:26).

And *kairos* is used in the same way in 12:14 (without article, after LXX Dan. 7:25; 12:7); *kairon kai kairous kai hēmisu kairou.* The dependence on Daniel shows that this stretch of time should be identified with the Danielic "last times."[8]

The original meaning of the *kairos* idea as a designation of a time appointed by God and filled with a special content glimmers through in 12:12 and 12:14. In the further course of investigation it will come out that the time of the dragon since his downfall (12:12) and the time of the woman (12:14) is the interval between the historical and the future Christ event. Thus *kairos* will be used for the whole time interval. A use of the word similar to that in Ephesians 5:16 and Colossians 4:5 lies before us. Here the *kairos,* which should be taken advantage of, can be nothing other than the present, qualified by the historical and future Christ event. This advantage-taking, that is, the saving use of the *kairos,* can occur only in the power of the divine wisdom. The same sense underlies Romans 12:11, if it is to be read with D and G as *tō kairō douleuontes* (instead of *tō kyriō*). Then *kairos* signifies the actual present point of the interval, appointed and distinguished by Christ.

The word *chronos* serves as the designation of a stretch of time (2:21; 6:11; 10:6; 20:3).

---

7 Reisner, *op. cit.,* p. 19.
8 Cf. Luke 4:25 and James 5:17, which connect the tradition of 1 Kings 17 and 18 with the 3½ times of the Danielic eschatology and understand them as a prototype of the eschatological, final period of evil.

In 2:21, the seductive false prophetess Jezebel is given by Christ a time to repent (*edōka chronon*), during which she is to make repentance if she would escape from the wrath of God.

In the same manner, *chronos* in 6:11 means a space of time appointed by God. It is designated as *mikros*. Its end is brought about by the *plērōthōsin kai hoi syndouloi*.

In 20:3, a short period of functioning is allowed the dragon after his chaining by God for a thousand years.

All three passages can best be translated with the idea of "delay." It pertains to a stretch of time whose end is appointed by God and is bound by a special condition.

Only the *chronos* passage in 10:6 has given frequent rise to variant interpretations. When the seventh trumpet resounds, it will be *hoti chronos ouketi estai*. It is questionable whether *chronos,* following the Greek usage, here denotes of itself abstract time or the temporal life. Does the Apocalyptist hope here for the conquest of time, the end of subjection to time?[9] By this time the use of the word in the other three passages should have warned against such excessive interpretations, which have no regard to the positive grounds in the whole of the Revelation which may be raised against such meaning. For, in the passage introduced by *alla,* "but," there is announced the condition for the expiration of a period of delay (*chronos ouketi estai*). The End comes, the mystery is fulfilled; therewith the delay has terminated and the seventh angel will sound his trumpet. And it is to be observed that it is precisely the End event of this seventh trumpet which is spoken of in temporal terminology (*all' en tais hēmerais . . .*). It cannot therefore be a question of the suspension of time. If the beginning of a timeless eternity were really expected here, the article would certainly have been used also (*ho chronos*). The expression is best taken, with Behm,[10] to mean "period of delay." The connection in which 10:6f.

9 So most recently Reisner, *op. cit., ad loc.,* who refers 10:6 to the end of the Old Testament period of revelation (corresponding to his interpretation of the trumpet visions as the period of the Old Testament and related to his identification of the End time and that which is beyond time): "The time which follows the Old Testament is properly no longer spoken of as time" (p. 94). Cf. also Beda's commentary, *ad loc.,* "the changeable variation of the world's times will cease with the last trumpet." Fr. Spitta, *Die Offenbarung des Johannes* (1889), pp. 101, 348, combines this passage with the four angels of 9:14ff. and understands it as the cessation of the whole sequence of time.

10 J. Behm, *Die Offenbarung des Johannes, NTD,* 4th ed. (1949), *ad loc.*

stands with Daniel 12:7 likewise speaks decisively for this interpretation.

The 3½ times expected in Daniel 12:7 draw attention to the definition of the *chronos* of the dragon in chapter 12, for here the "delay" is described precisely in terms of the Danielic 3½ times (cf. 12:12, 6, 14; 13:5). This suggests that we see in the *chronos* of 10:6 the same time span as in 12:12, where it is called *chronos mikros*. And this makes it possible to define the beginning and end points of the "delay." It begins with the historical Christ event (12:10-12) and ends with the Parousia (10:7) (cf. pp. 35ff. and 33f.).

All this renders unnecessary any dispute as to whether *chronos* means the time span between the seventh trumpet and the disclosure of the mystery, or between the present time of the Seer and the seventh trumpet, or between the present time of the Seer and the revelation of the mystery.[11]

In 9:5, a stretch of time is marked out in terms of months, *mēnas pente*. A plague of locusts will endure this long. The interpretation of this period, so far as I see, may be sought from six possible sources:

a) After the contemporary-popular interpretation, the time during which the swarm of locusts causes devastation lasts five months.[12]

b) The life time of the locusts is five months.[13]

c) Five months is a traditional round number for a long period of time.[14]

d) Five is the "half" number, the "broken number."[15]

e) Five months as the designation of the plague of locusts has its origin in astrology and means "until the end of the year." For in 9:3, scorpions are expected, and the number of the months from the scorpions to the last zodiacal signs of the year, until Pisces, yields exactly the desired number, five. Moreover, this helps to explain 9:6. The second half of the zodiac is the Hades

---

11 Cf. Bousset, *op. cit.,* pp. 310f.

12 Cf. Vitringa, Beda, Bengel, Düsterdieck, Joh. Weiss, Bousset, and others.

13 W. Hadorn, *Die Offenbarung des Johannes. Theologischer Handkommentar zum NT,* Vol. 18 (1928); Behm, Lohmeyer, Reisner, Lohse.

14 Lohmeyer.

15 Hengstenberg, Reisner.

side of the heavens and the guards of Hades turn away from
its gates all who are not appointed for entrance into it.[16]

f) Five months refers to the first phase of the Jewish War.[17]

From these six possibilities all manner of applications have been
sought, whether allegorical, church-, salvation-, or world-histori-
cal.[18]

In any case, the astrological origin of the expression is to be
denied as unproved, for certainly *hoi skorpioi tēs gēs* are expected
only as a simile of pain. No scorpions appear here; locusts do.
None of the remaining parts of the visions permit any direct references to astrology.

That "five" should be understood as the broken number is not
founded on anything here.[19] This interpretation would be more
quickly accepted if the half period of the year's total months, six,
stood here.[20] The third possibility appears, in my opinion, to be
most worth considering. It can also include the basic ideas of a)
and b). In 9:5 the particularly long duration of the devastation
should be emphasized. While natural swarms of locusts last only
a few days, these demonic swarms bring their torments throughout
the whole "time of locusts."[21]

A pertinent parallel to this is to be noted. With this expression
obviously something similar should be stated as is the case with
the "third" which appears in connection with the same series of
plagues (cf. 8:7-13; 9:18): The "third" indicates a physical limitation of the plagues; the five months a temporal limitation.

The number of months serves also to characterize the section
of time which is indicated by the Danielic 3½ *kairoi* (11:2; 13:5).
The change of expression appears to be premeditated here and not
to be derived from reference to two distinct patterns.[22] In both

---

16 Boll, *op. cit.*, pp. 71–73.

17 S. Giet, *op. cit.*, p. 154. This is nothing more than an accidental correspondence,
for a reference to the Jewish War is on other grounds impossible.

18 Cf. Reisner's latest "conjecture": He understands the five months as the half-time
of the revelation of salvation, the time of the Old Testament, or as the five hundred
years from the Babylonian exile.

19 "The broken number" is in the Revelation always 3½.

20 Corrected to this by Primasius.

21 The number five is similarly used in Matthew 25:15; Luke 12:6; 14:19; 16:28;
Matthew 14:17, 19; 16:9; 1 Corinthians 14:19. It is also employed for time in Genesis
7:24 (150 days) and certainly also in Luke 1:24.

22 Lohmeyer, *op. cit.*, p. 89.

passages the same conception is of course used for internally matching things, for the nations and their ruler, the beast. It will be seen that even the circumscription of the Danielic time with the number of days (11:3; 12:6) depends on an inner connection of these two passages.

Mēn serves also as a designation of a God-appointed point of time in 9:15. *Kata mēna* in 22:2 means "monthly."[23]

Hēmera, hēmerai, are used very frequently to designate points of time and periods of time.[24]

Hēmera as a designation of the daylight hours, as in 8:12 and 21:25, is theologically irrelevant.

Hēmerai is used in its Semitic sense, referring to a longer or shorter time span, whereby not so much the duration but that essential content of the time stands in the foreground:[25] "in the days of Antipas my witness," 2:13;[26] "in those days," 9:6;[27] "in the days of the trumpet call to be sounded by the seventh angel," 10:7.[28]

In 2:10, a period of tribulation "of ten days" is prophesied for the church.[29] As in Daniel 1:12, 14, the reference is simply to a short period of time (cf. Gen. 24:55; Judg. 6:25).

Hēmera is also used to indicate a precise point of time. Thus it is in 9:15, where a completely precise date, fixed by God, is spoken of. The word is used in 18:8 as an indication of fearsome brevity: "so shall her plagues come in a single day" (in contrast to the seemingly eternal permanence of Babylon's display of wealth).[30]

A longer definite period of time, the Danielic 3½ times, is also expressed in 11:3 and 12:6 by the number of days or simply designated as "the days of their prophesying" (11:6).

---

23 Cf. Strack and Billerbeck, *op. cit.,* 3:856.

24 As in the rest of the New Testament. Cf. O. Cullmann, *op. cit.,* I, 1; Delling, *TWB* 2:945–956; Jenni, *op. cit.,* p. 643.

25 See the examples from the New Testament in Delling, *Das Zeitverständnis,* pp. 65ff. For example, Matthew 2:1; Luke 1:80; Acts 7:45; 15:7; Hebrews 5:7.

26 The text is confused here, the original wording not certainly known.

27 The reference is to the period in which the event of the fifth trumpet is unveiled.

28 The period of the beginning of the End event.

29 The genitive is better attested than the accusative.

30 *Hōra* is certainly a secondary assimilation to 18:10, 17, 19.

In 11:9, 11, a shorter period is denominated by "three and a half days."[31]

Hēmera, together with *nux,* serves as a designation of the continuity of an event in 4:8; 7:15; 12:10; 14:11; 20:10.

A particular significance is given to *hēmera* where, after the manner of the Old Testament and Judaism, the beginning of the End event is designated,[32] as in 6:17 and 16:14.[33] The rest of the New Testament speaks in the same way as well, as in Matthew 7:22; Mark 13:32; Acts 2:20 (applied to Pentecost); 2 Timothy 1:12, 18; 4:8.

The expression *kuriakē hēmera* takes on a special significance in 1:10. John is taken by the Spirit on a "Lord's day." Without doubt we meet here a mention of the primitive Christian day of divine worship, the first day of the week.[34]

To denote a very short time or a point of time, the Revelation also uses *hōra.*

Without any special theological meaning, *hōra* indicates a period whose shortness should be emphasized: 17:12, the ten kings will come to power with the beast *mian hōran,* "for one hour."[35]

The sudden coming of an event is brought into prominence: 18:10, 17, 19 (Babylon is devastated *mia hōra*) and 11:13 (*en ekeinē tē hōra,* "at that hour there was a great earthquake").[36]

Hōra is also used as a designation of particular points of time. In 3:10 the "hour of trial," which will come over the entire world, is awaited. Therewith is designated the point of time of the last

---

31 On this, cf. pp. 39ff.

32 Cf. Joel 2:11, 31; Amos 5:18ff.; Zephaniah 1:15, 18. For verification from the Jewish literature, see Boussct, *Die Religion des Judentums,* p. 246, and especially Volz, *op. cit.,* pp. 163–165.

33 The textual variants are meaningless.

34 Cf. on the whole problem the monograph of W. Rordorf, *op. cit.,* especially pp. 203–212. Rordorf would derive the term *kuriakē hēmera* from the demonstrably earlier *kuriakon deipnon,* which had given its name to the day of worship (pp. 218ff.). That the day of the call vision is a day of worship ties in with the idea that the setting of the book as a whole is that of a heavenly worship service. Cf. thereto O. Piper, "The Apocalypse of John and the Liturgy of the Ancient Church," *Church History* (1951), pp. 10–22; S. Läuchli, *ThZ* 16 (1960), pp. 359–378; G. Delling "Zum gottesdienstlichen Stil der Johannes Apokalypse," *Novum Testamentum* 3 (1959), pp. 107–137. Simply to regard heavenly and earthly worship as parallel seems impossible to me (see the cautious judgment of Delling).

35 Accusative of time as in 3:3; 11:3; 9:5; 12:6.

36 Cf. Daniel 5:5; Joachim Jeremias, *"En ekeinē tē hōra (en) autō tē hōra,"* ZNW (1949), p. 216.

diabolical trial of the world, appointed by God to precede the End.[37] It is "that last encounter between God and the evil one which introduces the kingdom of God."[38]

In 9:15, the time of the administration of divine justice is defined by the term "hour," as is the case in 11:13. This last passage refers to the time of the End event and leads us to the next group of meanings for the "hour."

With *hōra,* as with *hēmera,* the coming of the time of the last judgment is particularly designated (the hour of the judgment and the harvest, 14:7, 15). Similarly, Mark 13:32 speaks of the hour which no one knows except the Father.[39]

A separate investigation is needed as well for the time designation in 14:13, *ap' arti.*[40] The punctuation of the sentence is doubtless correct: *makarioi hoi nekroi hoi en kuriō apothnēskontes ap' arti. nai . . .* It is questionable to which time point *ap' arti* should refer. Most commentators understand the "henceforth" as beginning with the time of the Seer,[41] which is characterized by the beginning of the great encounter of the church with the world.[42] Especially, it must be maintained that there is no compelling ground for referring *en kuriō apothnēskontes* to martyrdom. It is simply a matter (as in 1 Cor. 15:18 and 1 Thess. 4:16) of the faithful dead and dying.[43]

The solution propounded by Hadorn (that one will in the future rather die than live)[44] is beyond consideration because the idea of martyrdom is certainly not in mind. *Ap' arti* thus points to the beginning of a special time of salvation for those already dead in the Lord. However, it is then hard to see why a point of time such as that of the author, that is, the time of the writing of the Revelation or the time of the persecutions now beginning, should have given the Seer cause for such an important declaration. Only a

---

37 See pp. 62ff.
38 E. Lohmeyer, *Das Vater-Unser,* 2nd ed. (1947), p. 145.
39 On *hēmiōros,* cf. pp. 5f.
40 On the expression, cf. John 13:19; 14:7; Matthew 23:39; 26:29, 64.
41 A. Debrunner, *A Greek Grammar of the New Testament* (1962), § 12, 3, would read *aparti,* with A. Friedrichsen, as a vulgar form meaning "precise, definite" (without *nai,* with P47). This rare usage appears to me to be unlikely here.
42 Cf. Bousset, Hadorn, Behm.
43 Cf. pp. 104ff.
44 Hadorn, *op. cit., ad loc.,* cf. also Behm, *op. cit., ad loc.*

comparison with the use of *arti* in 12:10 will bring a solution. Here *arti* indicates the beginning of the time of eschatological salvation, the time of the historical Christ event. This specific time in the course of world history is designated by God as the beginning of the time of redemption, as the turning point of the world's history.[45]

Arti (= *nun*) thus can have a very pregnant theological meaning in connection with the historical Christ event and the associated apostolic proclamation.

This point of time has also brought a major turning point for "the dead who die in the Lord." Even their redemption has thereby been accomplished.[46] With the same expression, Jesus, in John 14:7, defines the new epoch, constituted by his presence. And thus the New Testament also speaks further of the "henceforth" in the sense of the present, qualified by the Christ event which endures until the Parousia.[47]

Arti is the "henceforth" as the decisive midpoint of time, as whose eyewitnesses and authoritative proclaimers the apostles live.[48] The apostolic consciousness of the author reveals itself in this *ap' arti* in 14:13; for he is an apostle who knows himself to be associated with the other apostles in the event of the End time. He has a portion with the other apostles "in the *ephapax* of the midpoint, although they otherwise already belong to the *ephapax* of the time of the church—as its foundation."[49]

Thus the Seer points with apostolic authority in 14:13 to the turning point of time in which he stands together with the primitive church.[50]

As the last of the terms for time in the Revelation there is found the term for "eternity": *aiōn*. The Old Testament and Judaism

---

45 "Henceforth" is here, as also in the rest of the New Testament, not only a boundary conception as in the Greek philosophers, but is itself a time of longer or shorter duration.

46 Cf. pp. 104ff.

47 Cf. Matthew 26:64; 1 Corinthians 13:12; 1 Peter 1:6, 8. "Henceforth" as a term for the decisive event of history is also used in John 12:31; 1 John 3:2; Romans 5:11.

48 Stählin, *TWB* 4:1099ff., gives too little emphasis to this belongingness of the apostle in the "henceforth" of the Christ event; hence his solution of Revelation 14:13 remains unsatisfactory also (4:1113).

49 Cullmann, *op. cit.*, II, 4.

50 Similarly Colossians 1:26; Ephesians 3:5; Romans 16:25f.; Hebrews 3:7, 13, 15.

understand aeon[51] as a designation for an immeasurably long duration of time. The later,[52] plural use of the word signifies no change in the understanding of time, only an alteration in the meaning of this one word.[53] The Revelation uses aeon in the formula *eis tous aiōnas tōn aiōnōn*[54] only in doxologies for God and Christ; it is further used as the designation of the duration of the lake of fire and the blessedness of the new creation.

Aeon (R.S.V.: "for ever and ever") stands in reference to God's and Christ's manner of existence in 1:18; 4:9; 10:6; 11:15; 15:7, and as a designation of the duration of the ascriptions of praise in 1:6; 5:13; 7:12.

Whether this formulary use of the plural *aiōnes* is to be understood in the Old Testament sense simply as an intensive plural,[55] or whether it is thought of as a series of aeons in the sense of "eras," cannot be determined with certainty.[56]

If the expression "the king of the aeons" (R.S.V.: "ages") in 15:3 should be original,[57] it would well be translated as "eternal king."[58] It could however also be thought of in the spatial or temporal sense, referring to the range of sovereignty of the "Almighty."

Aiōnios occurs once in the Revelation (14:6, said of the gospel). The meaning of this word must be determined on the basis of the aeon-concept.[59] Hence the adjective will simply mean "enduring an immeasurably long time" (cf. Rom. 16:25; 2 Tim. 1:9; Titus 1:2).

---

51 Cf. C. von Orelli, *op. cit.*, pp. 70ff.; W. Michaelis, *Versöhnung des Alls* (1950), pp. 41–48; E. Jenni, *op. cit.*, p. 644, and *Das Wort 'olam im AT* (1953).

52 Cf. Bousset, *op. cit.*, p. 501; O. Cullmann, *op. cit.*, I, 1.

53 In some late Jewish writings the conception of the *'olam haba* cannot be positively recognized; for instance, 2 Esdras 5:7, 11; 3:10; Syriac Baruch 3:6, 8, and other passages speak of an "end of time," meaning however no more than the cessation of the *'olam hazeh* (cf. Volz, *op. cit.*, p. 335). In Slavonic Enoch 65:7f., "the great aeon" appears to be thought of as timeless. The conception is uncertain, yet there appears to be here a genuine influence from hellenism (as also in the teaching that blessedness comes immediately after death; cf. Volz, *loc. cit.*) interwoven in the time idea.

54 The manuscript variants are of no consequence. The article is lacking only in 14:11, yet the conception remains the same.

55 Cf. E. Jenni, *op. cit.*, pp. 47–49.

56 Cf. my article "Aeon" in the *Biblisch-Historischen-Handwörterbuch*, ed. B. Reicke and L. Rost (1962), 1:103f.

57 The context indicates this to be improbable.

58 A Hebraic formation using the construct state; cf. H. Sasse, *TWB* 1:201; cf. also 1 Timothy 1:17.

59 O. Cullmann, *op. cit.*, p. 48, footnote 21, and Michaelis, *op. cit.*, p. 44, agree here. The LXX often renders *'olam* adjectively with *aiōnios* (cf. H. Sasse, *TWB* 1:208).

However, it can carry a special emphasis, since it refers in a special way to the coming aeon.[60] As a predicate of the grace of eschatological salvation, which is—like the coming aeon—of temporally unlimited duration, it then takes on the sense of a boundless extension into the future; it can even—except that it loses its temporal exactitude—actually take on the qualitative sense of "divine."[61] To be absolutely avoided, however, is the conception which Sasse works into the New Testament, the "eternity which transcends time."

For our passage in the Revelation, the last two meanings must be drawn in. The gospel (cf. pp. 103f.) is denoted as the message of eschatological salvation and has as such an abiding value.

Out of this survey of the temporal terminology of the Revelation certain deductions can be drawn:

a) The thought concerning time in itself, the temporality of human and general creaturely existence, is, in the Revelation as in the Old Testament, Judaism, and primitive Christianity, completely undeveloped. The expiration of time belongs to creaturely existence.

b) The individual points of time and epochs which characterize both salvation and world history as standing under God's guidance are very important. Integral to primitive Christian thought is the strong attachment of the individual portions and points of time to the person of Christ Jesus and his historical act of salvation.

c) Thus the temporal terms show that temporality is nowhere found as a problem or limitation of human existence. Indeed, the time categories can without restraint be employed even of God's mode of existence. The concept of an existence outside of time is totally foreign to the Revelation (as it is in the Old Testament, Judaism, and primitive Christianity). If thus an exegesis uses the Revelation's expressions in the sense of "beyond or

---

60 Cf. Hadorn, *op. cit.*, p. 203. Michaelis, *op. cit.*, p. 47, would simply translate it as "eschatological." To this group belongs the passages which Sasse, *TWB* 1:209, adduces under his Section 3.

61 Thereto belong the passages which Sasse, *TWB* 1:208f., adduces in his second section and the salvation conceptions which he includes in his third section. On this, cf. also L. Cerfaux, "L'Évangile éternel (Apoc. 14:6)," *ETL* 39 (1963), pp. 672–681.

above temporality, timelessness,"[62] it must be recognized that in so doing it says something contrary to the fundamental declarations about time in the Revelation.

2. THE ARRANGEMENT OF TIME

In order to gain insight into the outlook on time and history in the Revelation it is essential to become acquainted with the book's arrangement of time; precisely here is the decisive and specific element of the primitive Christian view of history displayed. The Christian view of history, through its dialectical, eschatological approach, distinguishes itself from the Jewish view, with its purely futuristic orientation, and from the Greek view, disinterested in history and its relationships. For the Christian conception sees the breaking in of the eschatological salvation as already present in a specific time segment of the historical past, and yet hopes for the realization of the eschatologically consummated kingdom in the future.[63] The question as to whether the Revelation is of Christian origin will thus be decided precisely by discovering whether it contains this Christian arrangement of time or allows itself to take the trail of another outlook.

The content of Revelation is the God-directed history of the present and the future (cf. 1:19, *ha eisin kai ha mellei genesthai meta tauta,* and 1:1, *ha dei genesthai en tachei*).[64]

The divine authorship of this history is clearly brought into prominence by the word *dei*.[65] The intent of the book is thus to reveal the plan of God with the history disclosing itself in the Seer's own time and which will come to its goal in the future.[66]

The divine plan is *mystērion tou theou,* thus wholly unintelligible to men (10:7). With the sound of the seventh trumpet the mystery

---

62 Cf., e.g., Lohmeyer and Reisner.

63 Cf. especially O. Cullmann, *op. cit.,* I, 5.

64 *Ha eisin* is certainly, in spite of Joh. Weiss, *op. cit., ad loc.,* to be translated as "what is." It is by no means indicated that *ha eisin* must refer only to the messages to the churches (Bousset, *Die Offenbarung Johannes, ad loc. et passim*), for even the messages themselves allude to the present time as well as to the future. *Ha eisin* means much more, as does *ha mellei genesthai,* for the whole book; and, as will be seen, this is of particular significance.

65 The textual variants in 1:19 also express this unchangeable divine character (cf. Primasius, *quae oportet fieri*).

66 The goal is particularly focused upon in 1:1, *ha dei genesthai en tachei.*

is consummated. This consummation can mean nothing other than the inbreaking of the kingdom of God. To this the context, 10:5f., points. Here the creator is spoken of, seemingly abruptly, but actually very meaningfully: God is the creator in primeval time and in the End time, the creator of the old and the new world. The commandment (10:8-11) however also points toward the End event, the commandment to proclaim the prophetic message of the mystery once again; for the urgency of this proclamation springs from the fact that only a short period is available until the End.

The content of the whole book is therefore God's plan of salvation, which, though obscured from men, defines and illuminates both the actual present in the moment of receiving the vision and the whole future.

This plan has become intelligible to the Seer through *apokalypsis*. The conception cannot be used solely as a synonym for the Parousia[67] nor in a purely formal sense of "receipt of revelation," nor only in the sense of "content of that which is revealed."[68] The Revelation uses it as the content of the word of God which John encounters because the Seer himself is conscious of the plan of salvation, the divine mystery, imparted as a whole and in which all other individual instances of revelation (*apokalypseis*) must take place.[69]

The more precise definition of this *apokalypsis* as *Iēsou Christou* gives us now a point of reference for the Revelation's arrangement of time and its understanding of history. That Jesus Christ is the revealer of the plan of salvation shows that the present and future referred to in 1:1, 19, is defined and designated by Christ Jesus, the one who in a particular past time has consummated the decisive act of salvation. This determining of Christ's basic function in the Revelation excludes the idea that in the connection of the *apokalypsis* with Jesus Christ it should be characterized as "timeless."[70] Much more there must be borne in mind the preciseness of the

---

67 Cf. 1 Corinthians 1:7; 2 Thessalonians 1:7; 1 Peter 1:7, 13; for the inbreaking of the kingdom, Romans 2:5; 8:19.

68 Cf. 1 Corinthians 14:6, 26; 2 Corinthians 12:1, 7; Galatians 2:2; Ephesians 1:17.

69 Cf. thereto especially Ephesians 3:3, which likewise designates the *apokalypsis* by *mystērion*, which contains the plan of salvation.

70 Lohmeyer, *Die Offenbarung des Johannes, ad loc.*

portion of time referred to in the Revelation by the historical act of Christ.

Which part of time since Christ does the Revelation intend to portray? Only the final portion, from the Seer's viewpoint purely futuristic (prior to the End) and including the End itself, or the whole period between the two appearances of Christ?

We gather from the investigation of the construction of the Revelation that the sections 6:1–8:1; 8:2–11:19; 12:1–14:20; 15:1–16:21; 17:1–19:10 deal with the time before and up to the Parousia. They shall now be looked at more closely.

It is most clear that the time span which the Apocalyptist includes in his visions is recognizable in chapters 12–14. The great vision of the twelfth chapter is connected with older traditions by many scenic elements. But the whole drama is so conceived that it will not allow itself to be derived easily from any sort of prototype. Since Gunkel and Bousset there have been frequent fruitless attempts to establish an influence from a pagan myth.[71] In more recent work there has been much more freedom from this effort and the anchoring of the individual scenic elements in the Old Testament recognized and emphasized.[72] And most scholars have referred to a passage from the Qumran Hodayoth whose interpretation is certainly much disputed, 1QH 3:7-12.[73] The psalmist speaks here of his distress, which overtakes him as a "woman is overcome with pains at the birth of her firstborn." Then the pain-filled birth of a child is spoken of. Because the psalm expresses a view of the eschatological calamity, it must have the birth of the messianic time in mind here,[74] described in words taken from the Old Testament prophets.[75] Certainly, the woman here is representative of the

---

71 See especially P. Prigent, *op. cit.,* pp. 120–135; A. Feuillet, *L'Apocalypse, État de la question,* pp. 91–98.

72 A. Feuillet, "Le Cantique des Cantiques et l'Apocalypse," *Recherches de Science Religieuse* 49 (1961), pp. 321–353, and "Le Messie et sa Mère d'après le chapitre 12 de l'Apocalypse," *RB* 1 (1959), pp. 54–86, sees a parallel between 12:1 and Song of Solomon 6:10 and the Old Testament passages which speak of a woman in labor. On the connection with Genesis 3:6, cf. L. Cerfaux, "La Vision de la Femme et du Dragon de l'Apocalypse," *ETL* 31 (1955), pp. 29, 3.

73 Cf. Feuillet's essays in the previous note.

74 The plural in verse 11 speaks against identifying the newborn child with the Messiah; cf. G. Hinson, "Hodayoth 3:6–18: In What Sense Messianic?" *Revue de Qumran* 2 (1960), pp. 183–204.

75 See A. S. van der Woude, *Die messianischen Vorstellungen der Gemeinde von Qumran* (1957), pp. 144–156, and J. Maier, *Die Texts vom Toten Meer* (1960), II, pp.

community (cf. Isa. 26:17ff. and other passages).[76] Over against her stands another woman, "pregnant with illusion," representing a community with a futile eschatological hope, who is destined to perish (cf. Isa. 59:4f.). 1QH 3:7-12 thus yields nothing more than the Old Testament passages basic to the portrayal of the birth of times of salvation or disaster.

But the key passages from the Old Testament are only individual stones of a mosaic worked into the scene. The event, the drama, which plays itself out before our eyes, is to be found neither in the Old Testament nor in the Jewish apocalypses. It appears to me that by far the closest thing to Revelation 12 is the LXX setting of Isaiah 26:17–27:1.

Here, the community of Israel in its time of eschatological distress is seen in the figure of the woman who cries out in her birth pangs. While according to the usual interpretation of the Masoretic text in verse 18 a bringing forth of "wind," that is, the shattering of the eschatological hopes, is spoken of,[77] the LXX interprets it messianically as referring to the birth of the "beloved": *houtōs egenēthēmen to agapētō sou*.[78] The LXX text yields a striking agreement in the following motifs:

1. The woman cries out in the pain of the messianic birth (Isa. 26:17; Rev. 12:2).
2. The manifestation of God's wrath follows after a short time (Isa. 26:20), transferred in Revelation 12:12 to the dragon (also here the short period is emphasized).[79]

72ff. Here also is a criticism of the thesis of O. Betz, "Das Volk der Kraft," *NTS* 5 (1958), pp. 67–75, and previously "Die Geburt der Gemeinde durch den Lehrer," *NTS* 3 (1957), pp. 312–326, which would identify the woman with the "teacher" of the community and the child with the nation (after Isa. 9:6).

76 See especially the above-mentioned works of van der Woude and Maier.

77 O. Procksch, *Jesaja I, Kommentar zum AT,* ed. E. Sellin, Vol. 9 (1930), pp. 324–330, reads *kemo yoledah* instead of *yaladnu* and connects *ruach* with *yeshu'ot,* as in the LXX. "We cry out like a woman giving birth. The Spirit has not wrought deliverance on the earth . . ." "The protasis to verse 18 points not to the condition after the birth, but prior to it, and indicates a reference, not to the birth of wind, but to a genuine birth."

78 J. Ziegler (*Göttinger Septuaginta,* Vol. 14), *Isaias* (1939), p. 212, would read in verse 18 (*pneuma sōtērias sou*) an unattested *ouk* in place of *sou,* in spite of the MT. But the LXX text certainly had a Hebrew original somewhat similar to that of 1QIsa, where *yshw'tk* is read (M. Burrows, *The Dead Sea Scrolls of St. Mark's Monastery* I [1950]).

79 On the "little while," cf. the observations of A. Strobel, "Untersuchungen zum eschatologischen Verzögerungsproblem auf Grund der spätjüdisch urchristlichen Geschichte von Hab. 2:2ff.," *Supplements to Novum Testamentum* (1961), p. 86.

3. During this time the community is hidden (Isa. 26:20);[80] according to Revelation 12:6 it is protected in the wilderness.

4. In the little apocalypse of Isaiah, there is also found the dragon (Leviathan, the serpent, Rev. 12:9!), Isaiah 27:1, who is defeated (cf. the war motif in Rev. 12:7-12; 5:5).

It is quite conceivable that we find here the bud which has blossomed out in Revelation 12 in astounding multiplicity of detail. Complete certainty is, of course, not attainable.[81] But the evident attachment with the conceptions of the Old Testament suggests the probability of the conjecture offered above.

The vision of the twelfth chapter is clearly composed of three parts.[82] First, the great sign in heaven is portrayed: the woman, distinguished as being clothed with the sun, with the moon under her feet, and wearing a crown of twelve stars, gives painful birth to the ruler "who is to rule all the nations with a rod of iron." The great dragon intends to devour the child, but he is rescued out of the dragon's clutches and caught up to God's throne. The woman flees into the wilderness and is protected there during the time of the End. The second scene directs attention again up to heaven (vss. 7-12). Michael and his angels throw the dragon out of heaven down to the earth. The victory is celebrated in the hymn in 12:10-12 and used to signify the eschatological victory of God and his Christ. In the third section, the earth is again the scene of action. The dragon, now cast down to the earth, engages the woman in battle, but she is preserved by the divine intervention. Her flight to the wilderness, already spoken of at the end of the first section, is now described more precisely. There in the wilderness her existence is safeguarded. In his anger, the dragon finally rushes off after the other children of the woman.

We shall have frequent opportunity to enter into the details of

---

80 Here it is "tacitly assumed that the place of refuge is not affected by the destructive work of Yahweh" (O. Plöger, *Theokratie und Eschatologie* [1959], pp. 85f.).

81 The Seer could very well have drawn the raw material itself, which he uses in order to deliver his message, from a mythical history of the birth and rescue of the divine child. The material taken over would, in any event, have been completely reorganized. Until now however a clear parallel has nowhere been found.

82 See especially W. Foerster, "Die Bilder in Offenbarung 12f. und 17f.," *Theol. Stud. u. Krit.* 104 (1932), pp. 279–310, and A. Roets, "Een vrouw omkleed met de zon . . . Maria en de Kerk in de Apocalypse 12," *Collationes Brugenses et Gandavenses* 8 (1962), pp. 332–360.

the chapter. Here we are primarily interested in the birth of the child. Undoubtedly the male child (a Hebraizing expression, cf. Jer. 20:15) indicates the Messiah who, according to Psalm 2:9, will rule the nations. But there is a question not easily answered: Does the text speak of the historical birth of Jesus or of an eschatological-futuristic birth (the Parousia), of a time-suspending recapitulation and manifestation of the historical birth of Jesus "before all the world," whereby "the eschatological future and the historical past and present serve the function of a timeless religious meaning,[83] or even of the crucifixion and resurrection, portrayed as the painful birth and elevation to the throne?[84]

It must be clearly noted that the mother of the Messiah, initially seen in heaven, finds herself on earth with the child and is there attacked by the dragon and rescued in the desert. And from the earth the child is taken up into heaven. The assault on God's community is also begun with the account of the birth and taking up of the Messiah. And one must not forget that with Satan's overthrow, portrayed as a consequence of the messianic event, a primitive Christian viewpoint has been absorbed which is inseparably bound up with the earthly life of Jesus (Lk. 10:18).

As in Philippians 2:5-11, all statements about the details of the Incarnation of Jesus which might be accessible to the historical observer are avoided, and only that hidden, underlying meaning of the event which is pertinent to salvation history is made apparent.

The abbreviated form in which the whole Christ event is set forth is quite singular, especially the omission of the crucifixion. However, it is worth noting at this point that the same thing is found in the brief hymn in 1 Timothy 3:16. This passage begins with the revelation in the flesh and concludes with the taking up in glory, but lacks any mention of the death of Jesus. But at the same time the believers' confidence in victory, as shown in the interpretive hymn (12:10-12), is traced back to Jesus' historical act of sacrifice. Thus the victory of God is seen here clearly to be associated with the submission of the slain Lamb. This is typical

---

83 E. Lohmeyer, *op. cit.,* pp. 108–110.
84 A. Feuillet, *op. cit.,* pp. 54–86. Against this is the fact that it is the mother who suffers, not the child.

of the whole Revelation. In this manner the ruling Lion of the tribe of Judah is identified with the Lamb: the Lamb that is slain is at the same time the bearer of the seven horns, the symbol of power, and the seven spirits of God, the fullness of the Holy Spirit. With metaphorical language: The Revelation proclaims again and again the paradox that the suffering and dying Christ is the victor. This paradox characterizes the Christ event set forth in the twelfth chapter: "she brought forth a male child, one who is to rule all the nations with a rod of iron, but her child was caught up to God and to his throne." Thus the enthronement of the messianic ruler is tied in with the birth in a singular manner, Christ speaking of the same thing in the letter to the church of Laodicea (3:21). This ruler is the child who is born into the arena of the dragon's power and whose enthronement is a snatching away from the threat of death. This conception of the removal and ascent to the throne appears to stand in close connection with the Old Testament thought (stemming from the eschatological myth) of Yahweh's enthronement, tied in turn to the idea of the ascension of Yahweh. Here the conception is transferred to Christ (cf. Ps. 47:5, 8).[85] Obviously, the primitive Christian message of the Easter victory and the ascension of Jesus stands behind this for John.

The victory and coming to authority of Christ is yet hidden from the world, a reality only for the faithful who are bound to the heavenly Christ. The puzzling brevity with which the historical Christ event is shown is thus explained by the metaphorical formulation of this paradoxical truth about Christ.[86]

From all this comes the following result: Revelation 12–14 begins with the historical Christ event and ends with the Parousia and obviously gives an explanation for the entire intermediary time. That gives now the possibility of confirming the interpretation of the Danielic number 3½ (and its variations) in the Revelation. In Daniel it designates the duration of the last stretch of time directly

---

85 Cf. H. Gressmann, *Der Ursprung der israelitisch-jüdischen Eschatologie* (1905), pp. 294–301; *Der Messias* (1929), pp. 212ff. Judaism also speaks of an ascension of the Messiah at the end of the messianic time, e.g., Syriac Baruch 30:1.

86 That only the beginning and end of the history of Christ is mentioned, the intervening events being passed over, suggests a Semitism, cf. J. Jeremias, *The Parables of Jesus*, p. 148.

prior to the great final judgment and the appearing of the Son of Man (Dan. 7:13, 26). In the Revelation it is no longer meant concretely, as it is in Daniel,[87] while the great distinction from Daniel remains in the new designation of the point of departure of the last time before the End. Daniel, and with it the Jewish apocalyptists, takes the actual point of time of the writing of the book[88] as the point of departure of the last time because he is convinced that he will witness God's world plan in his own decisive hour.[89] However, the refusal of these prophecies to be more specific is always obvious, so that the "later apocalyptic becomes cautious in its numbers in comparison with Daniel."[90] The new thing found in the Revelation (and in the whole of primitive Christianity) is that it recognizes positively the precise point of the beginning of the final time, this on the basis of the most infallible divine attestation through the appearance of Jesus Christ on earth in the past (12:6).[91] The Danielic number thus serves in the Revelation as a designation of the intermediary time. This last time is the time of the *gynē* (12:6, 14) and the two witnesses (11:3), although it is also the time of the beast and the *ethnē* who believe in him[92] (11:2; 13:5). In these passages it is always the same End time between the two Parousias that is meant.

In 11:2 is found the point of departure for the 3½ times, the End time, the *patein* of Jerusalem,[93] the desecration by the nations.[94] The inner ground of the profanation is, according to Revelation 11:8, the crucifixion of Jesus.[95]

---

87 In Daniel the half year-week is certainly understood literally; cf. the dislocation of the calculation caused by the failure of the End to occur: Daniel 9:24ff.; 12:7, 11, 12 (see Volz, *op. cit.*, pp. 142ff., 145; Bousset, *Die Religion des Judentums*, pp. 246–249).

88 In the author's program of history it is clear that he looks ahead "prophetically" from an assumed, earlier standpoint.

89 Cf. Apocalypse of Baruch 59:8; 56:2; 20:6; 14:1.

90 Cf. 2 Esdras 6:7f.; Volz, *op. cit.*, p. 146.

91 The whole New Testament view of the End time conforms to this; cf. especially 1 John 2:18; Cullmann, *op. cit.*, II, 3.

92 Cf. II, 1, and III, 2 and 3. Cf. also the significant work of W. G. Kümmel on the intermediary time anticipated even by Jesus (*op. cit.*, pp. 25ff., 64ff.).

93 Cf. III, 3.

94 Even the synoptic tradition knows this motif (Lk. 21:24). There is a striking late Jewish parallel which runs from the destruction of Jerusalem for the seventy year-weeks of Jeremiah to the End and sets in motion the final premessianic time of the surrender to the Gentiles, the Danielic 3½ times: Midrash on Psalm 10, "They shall be given into his (the oppressor's) hand, Daniel 7:25. Can it be for ever? The scriptural teaching says: a time and two times and a half time, Daniel 7:25." Cf. Strack and Billerbeck, *op. cit.*, IV:1004–1009.

95 Cf. pp. 96ff.

Thus both of these starting points in chapters 11 and 12 stand in the innermost connection, they clearly synchronize; the End time begins with the Christ event. We shall later see that 11:1-13 concludes the intermediary time with a vision of the End. Thus even this view of the temple and the witnesses in chapter 11 includes an overview of the whole time interval.

The Danielic number is also used in 13:5. There the beginning of the last time is established by the appearance of the beast. We shall see in III, 2, that even this point of time synchronizes with the Christ event.

With this investigation of the point of departure of the End time in the Revelation it seems to me that we have found an important means toward the understanding of the whole book. It remains from this to investigate whether all the visions prior to 19:10 speak of the End time so understood.

As a matter of fact, the introductory vision of the central, apocalyptic section of the book discloses the same outlook. Here the ruler of the world holds in his right hand a scroll sealed with seven seals.[96] The unsealing brings about the occurrence of the final events, as 6:1–8:1 shows.[97] The scroll obviously contains the outcome of the End time, that outcome lying in God's hand (cf. 1:1).[98]

H. P. Müller has shown the proper way to explain the whole

---

96 On the form of the scroll, cf. particularly F. Spitta, *op. cit.*, pp. 280f. Whether the visionary could describe the much-discussed technical details themselves is, however, doubtful. The scroll is described in words from Ezekiel 2:9f., indicating that the original reading of the text was probably *esōthen kai opisthen*; see A. Schlatter, *op. cit.*, p. 61; J. Schmid, *Studien zur Geschichte des griechischen Apokalypse-Textes*, Part 1 (1955), pp. 74f.; and E. Lohse, *ZNW* 52 (1961), pp. 124f. Cf. also A. Deissmann, *Licht vom Osten* (1923), p. 28.

97 Sealing a book indicates that its contents remain under lock and key; unsealing indicates that its contents are made visible, Isaiah 29:11f., Revelation 10:4; 22:10. This means in the case of chapter 5 that the content comes to pass with the unsealing. Nothing in the text suggests that there is first a preparatory vision whose events must occur right after the opening of the seventh seal (so Allo, *op. cit.*, pp. 68ff.). That the martyrs would have no more cause for lamenting were the judgment already in progress does not suggest such a thing, because the seal visions involve only a judgment within history, not the final judgment. That the four winds of chapter 7 are not let loose after the sixth seal has no significance here, for chapter 7 is an independent interlude.

98 Cf. Psalm 139:16; 56:8; Daniel 10:21; 2 Esdras 6:20: the plagues of the End time will be introduced by the opening of books *ante faciem firmamenti*. The proposals of O. Roller, "Das Buch mit 7 Siegeln," *ZNW* 36 (1937), pp. 98–113, referring to a "certificate of guilt," and of W. Sattler, *ZNW* 21 (1922), pp. 43–53, referring to a "book of life" (so also F. Nötscher, "Himmlische Bücher und Schicksalsglaube im Qumran," *Revue de Qumran* 1 [1959], pp. 405ff.) are not satisfactory in this connection; cf. G. Bornkamm, *Die Komposition der apokalyptischen Visionen in der Offenbarung Johannes. Studien zur Antike und Urchristentum*, II (1959), pp. 204–222. The nearest comparison lies

scene.[99] He draws attention to a pattern of commissioning traceable in the ancient oriental literature (so in the already mentioned myth, of the plunder of the tablets of destiny by the bird Zu) and which appears in the Old Testament in Isaiah 6:8f. and 1 Kings 22:19-22.

The latter text shows the common pattern especially clearly: 1. the question of finding someone to take on the task; 2. the perplexity of the assembly; 3. the designation of one who is ready and able to undertake the task. This pattern includes all the details of the text of Revelation 5 and explains them better than does the often cited ancient enthronement ceremonial.[100]

The high position of the one who alone is able to carry out the divine plan successfully lies in his victory (5:5). In the interpretive hymn *enikēsen,* used absolutely, refers to the sacrificial death of the Lamb (5:9f.). Therefore the victor is also designated as the lamb who had been slain.[101] His sacrificial death[102] carries with it a universal significance for the whole of world history and indicates the beginning of the final period itself, the End time.

The situation of the scroll in chapter 5 is wholly similar to that

---

in the gods' tablets of destiny, which indicate world dominion (appropriate texts are found in H. Gressmann, *Altorientalische Texte zum Alten Testament,* 1926, pp. 141ff., and J. B. Pritchard, *Ancient Near Eastern Texts Relating to the OT* [1955], pp. 110ff., to which T. Holtz, *op. cit.,* p. 36, refers).

99 H. P. Müller, "Die himmlische Ratsversammlung," *ZNW* 54 (1963), pp. 254–267.

100 H. P. Müller, *op. cit.,* p. 259.

101 Whether the lamb as a messianic figure was already known in Judaism remains uncertain. It appears to me however to be thoroughly possible. Testament of Joseph 19:8ff. (whose Armenian version is perhaps original): The idea of the lamb possibly connects with the Old Testament representations of Israel as God's flock (cf. also Eth. Enoch 89), is then applied to individuals (David, Samuel, Moses), and in this way has become associated with the Messiah. Thus the Messiah as the representative of Israel would be "the lamb" in contrast to the wild beasts (heathen) whom he defeats. For further discussion, cf. M. Philonenko, *Les interpolations chrétiennes des testaments des 12 patriarches et les manuscrits de Qumran* (1960), pp. 29f.; J. Jeremias, *TWB* 1:342ff.; the excursis in Lohmeyer, *op. cit., ad loc.;* and T. Holtz, *op. cit.,* pp. 39ff.

102 Cf. 1 Peter 1:19; John 1:29, 36; 1 Corinthians 5:7 (where Christ is termed the paschal lamb, which corresponds with the Johannine tradition of the death of Jesus, John 19:36). To connect the figure of the lamb with astral speculations about the ram (Boll, *op. cit.,* pp. 44–46), is, on linguistic and material grounds, extremely doubtful, for in Jewish-Greek usage the word occurred only with the sense of "lamb," while the seven horns may be explained from Old Testament conceptions (the horn as a figure of power: Num. 23:22; Deut. 33:17; Ps. 75:5, etc.). In the Revelation this figure of power is associated with the number seven, the symbol of totality. This figure becomes a symbol of omnipotence (on the paradox: lamb = omnipotence, cf. above). T. Holtz, *op. cit.,* pp. 44–50, would understand the apocalyptic lamb as the paschal lamb, which has support in the paschal typology of 15:3f. And the blood of the paschal lambs makes atonement (J. Jeremias, *The Eucharistic Words of Jesus* [1955], pp. 146ff.). O. Cullmann, *The Christology of the NT* (1963), pp. 71f., sees the passover thought operative in Isaiah 53 and relates this chapter to the expressions involving the lamb in the New Testament.

of the *biblaridion* in chapter 10. Chapters 10:1–11:13 portray an independent interval as does chapter 7. The little scroll, which holds together the whole vision in chapter 10 (cf. 10:2, 8-11), includes the content of the announcement of the mystery of God (10:7) ordered in 10:8-11. The mystery is God's plan of salvation for the whole world.[103] The little scroll contains thus a recapitulation[104] of the plan of salvation for the whole End time already laid out several times.

But where now is the content of the little scroll to be found? In order to answer this question attention must be paid to a formal characteristic of the "intervals" in the Revelation. The interval between the sixth and seventh seals (chapter 7)—as also the interval between the sixth and seventh trumpets (10:1–11:13)—is in two parts. Whereas in chapter 7 a clear, inner homogeneity of both parts has been established, it must be investigated whether both divisions of chapters 10 and 11 are really tied together. Actually, 11:1-13, which contains—as we have seen—a summary of the whole interval, lends itself most naturally to be understood as a display of the contents of the little scroll of chapter 10 and as the carrying out of the command of 10:11. All attempts to find the content of the little scroll anywhere other than in chapter 11 will prove arbitrary. The events of the eleventh chapter are joined organically to the heavenly announcements from chapter 10 on, so that it is not to be doubted that they portray the latter chapter's content. And the designation of the content of the *biblaridion* as "sweet and bitter"[105] lends itself to be understood as descriptive of the events of chapter 11.[106] For this reason all efforts at source criticism of chapters 10 and 11 are superfluous. The Seer has given a survey of the End time on several occasions already and means to do it here once more.

Between the opening of the sixth and seventh seals there slips in the intervening chapter 7, now to be more closely considered

---

103 Therefore the pleonastic manner of expression in 10:11. Cf. G. Bornkamm, *TWB* 4:830.
104 Cf. the *palin* in 10:11, E. Lohse, *Die Offenbarung des Johannes*, p. 56.
105 10:9f. Cf. Ezekiel 3:1ff. Sweetness and bitterness are symbols of grace and judgment (cf. K. L. Schmidt, *op. cit.*, pp. 161–177).
106 See pp. 96ff.

(and here again only according to the special viewpoint of the arrangement of time).[107]

That 7:1ff. not only brings out more clearly the event of the sixth seal but also introduces something new is made evident by the introductory formula *meta touto*.[108]

The interval begins with the portrayal of the four winds which are held back until the completion of the sealing of the 144,000. The effect of the winds is destructive (7:2), the consequence of God's wrath.[109] The introduction of the four winds with the article shows that they point to a particular, known tradition. The number four, as a conception of totality[110] indicates that its effect is universal, extending over land and sea. That trees are also mentioned can be connected with traditional conceptions; they are "visible signs of calm or storm."[111]

The passage bears a strong resemblance to Daniel 7:2, where the same sort of expression is used of the breaking in of the eschatological events.[112] Revelation 7:1 can thus be understood only as an introduction to the story of the End.

That nothing more happens in connection with the loosing of the winds does not require an explanation on the basis of a special source.[113] The context indeed gives no occasion for this, because the content of the wind's effect is well displayed in the other portrayals of the last times. The inner homogeneity of the winds with the trumpet visions is even expressly mentioned in 9:4. Further-

---

107 Cf. III, 3 and 4.

108 So also Lohmeyer, *op cit., ad loc.*, and others.

109 Similar thoughts and conceptions are found in Jeremiah 49:36; Eth. Enoch 34–36; 60:11f.; 69:22; 76.

110 Cf. Boll, *op. cit.*, pp. 20ff., and Gunkel, *Zum religionsgeschichtlichen Verständnis des NT, FRL*, 3rd ed. (1930), pp. 45f.

111 Lohmeyer, *op. cit.*, p. 65.

112 Theodotion likewise uses the article here: *hoi tessares anemol*. Bousset, *Die Offenbarung Johannes*, p. 280, points also to the affinity of our passage with the pseudo-Johannine Apocalypse 25:2; Syriac Apocalypse of Peter and Sibylline Oracles 8:203f. (Cf. also Bousset, *Der Antichrist* [1895], p. 165.) Also in the Mandaean texts the same sort of conceptions are met: in the introduction to a speech by Johana, it is said, "The four winds of the house (the world) take themselves off on wings and blow not" (Johannine Book 84; Ginza 203). In the Johannine Book 222, it is said of the time prior to the world's creation, "The storms became silent and they remain in the desert places of the world." It relates certainly to widespread oriental mythic materials about the primeval time and the End time, which here in the Revelation are taken up as metaphors for the eschatological winds, "which shall be loosed at the end of the world" (Bousset, *Die Offenbarung Johannes*, p. 280).

113 Bousset, Spitta, and others.

more, *achri sphragisōmen* (7:3) implicitly points to the letting loose of the winds: they will blow as soon as the sealing is ended. In the second scene of the interval the entry of this eschatological event is presupposed, for those seen come "out of the great tribulation" (7:14).

The End time also in chapter 7 is to be defined according to no other scheduling principle than that already presented. Here again the sole concern is the intermediary time as a whole. The parallelism with the intermediate period in 10–11 points to this as well. Confirmation of this comes from a further observation:

The angel who brings the "seal of the living God" comes *apo anatolēs hēliou* (v. 1., *anatolōn*). The east, the place where the sun rises (and therewith light and life),[114] is in Jewish thought the place from whence in a special way God's manifestations are expected: Paradise is there (Gen. 2:8; Enoch 32:3[115]); from the east God himself stirred up Cyrus (Isa. 41:2) and from the east "the glory of the God of Israel" comes to the temple (Ezek. 43:2). From the east also the divine judgment breaks in as a storm and destroys the godless (Mekilta of Exod. 14:21[116]).

And so in a special manner the messianic king of light is awaited in connection with some such conceptions (originally from astral myths) about the rising of the sun.[117] From this comes the explanation of the significant fact that the "star" of Numbers 24:17 becomes the "morning star" from the east in Revelation 22:16.[118] Certainly the coming of the angel out of the east points to this messianic connection, for "it does not suit the tenor of the apoca-

---

114 Cf. Boll, *op. cit.*, p. 20, and the summary in Bousset, *op. cit., ad loc.*
115 Cf. Spitta, *op. cit.*, pp. 317f., with further examples. See also F. Nötscher, *Zur theologischen Terminologie der Qumrantexte* (1956), pp. 92ff., 134–148 (on terminology involving light).
116 Cf. Volz, *op. cit.*, p. 319.
117 Cf. Sibylline Oracles 3:652; Erbes' commentary, *ad loc.;* Volz, *op. cit.*, pp. 209f.
118 Cf. Revelation 2:28, where the faithful are promised the morning star as an eschatological salvation gift, which can be explained as none other than Christ himself. (Cf. the same manner of expression in the Gospel of John, where the eschatological blessings of salvation, *zōē, phōs*, are identified with the person of Christ. In this outlook John's Gospel and the Revelation are in the deepest agreement with Paul, in whose terminology the same situation is expressed as *zē de emoi christos*, Gal. 2:20.) The aftereffect of the conception in the ancient Christian directing of prayer to the east is interesting, as it developed especially in contrast to the Jewish *qibla* toward Jerusalem. (Cf. Erik Peterson, "Die geschichtliche Bedeutung der jüdischen Gebetsrichtung," *ThZ* [1947].)

lyptic notions if one speaks of the east only as the region of light and salvation."[119]

The angel out of the east brings the mark of salvation, which, according to 14:1, consists of the name of God and the Lamb. The 144,000 who are sealed stand accordingly under the mark of Jesus, who has wrought salvation through his death. The seal, the mark of messianic salvation, has its root in the historical Christ event. Thus the representation of the sealed displays the actuality of the members of Christ's congregation in the End time.

It remains for us yet to study the sevenfold series of 8:2–11:19. Even it can be understood only as a portrayal of the entire End time. For again, the series terminates with a portrayal of the End;[120] in the same way, the introduction of the events through the sounding of the trumpets points to this understanding. The trumpet was previously used in the Old Testament as a sign of a special eschatological act of salvation;[121] in Judaism it proclaims "God's appearing,"[122] and calls for the general resurrection of the dead and for redemption.[123] In the New Testament, the trumpet points toward the beginning of the End.[124] In John's Revelation, the sound of the eschatological trumpet resounds, not initially at the Parousia, but in the present, which achieves its position as the End time through the presence of the risen Son of Man (1:10; cf. 4:1). The time disclosed by the sound of the eschatological trumpet is the End time between the Parousias of Jesus Christ. The cosmic catastrophe of the first four trumpets stands wholly within the range of the Jewish and primitive Christian expectations of the End.[125] But also the demonic oppressions of the fifth and sixth trumpets correspond to the Jewish outlook on the End time.[126]

---

119 Spitta, *op. cit., ad loc.* The references of Boll, *op. cit.,* pp. 48–50, to star-angel magic and of Lohmeyer, *op. cit.,* p. 28, to Holy Spirit-Ishtar are too artificial and find no support in the text. Cf. Foerster, *TWB* 1:502.

120 Cf. p. 8.

121 Isaiah 27:13; Joel 2:1.

122 Volz, *op. cit.,* p. 346.

123 Apocalypse of Ezra 4:36; cf. the Samaritan eschatology and the daily call for prayer in Shemone 10: "Blow the great trumpets for our liberation."

124 1 Corinthians 15:52; 1 Thessalonians 4:16; Matthew 24:31. Cf. Bousset, *Der Antichrist,* p. 166.

125 See the synoptic apocalypses and the passages which Volz, *op. cit.,* pp. 152ff., cites.

126 Cf. for example Syriac Baruch 27:9: ". . . and in the eighth period many appearances and demonic encounters." To admit (as does Lohmeyer, *op. cit., ad loc.*)

There is now no reason at all to understand these visions of the End time differently from the others. A comparison with the bowl visions will directly demand our solution.[127]

The mention of the sealing in the fifth trumpet vision (9:4) shows that the trumpet visions occur in the same time as that of which chapter 7 speaks; thus, in the intermediary time. And there is to be seen immediately at hand in 8:2–11:19 a vision of the End time between the Parousias.

A new point of view begins with chapters 15–16, the bowl visions. They bring a further scheduling of time and history. In them the final temporal period before the End is portrayed. That chapters 15–16 include this final time and do not simply put forth a repetition and recapitulation of the other series is clear for the following reasons:

The events of the seven bowls are called "the last." There is no reason to disregard the purely temporal meaning. *Eschatai* is more closely defined by *etelesthē:* God's wrath is completed through them and is coming to its end.

At the beginning of these bowl events there is already a host of Christian dead dwelling in heaven who are praised as conquerors.[128] For this reason, we see that the time reference is to the last part of the intermediary time. Moreover, it must be observed that the usual "name of God with threefold time-reference"[129] is encountered in an altered form in the hymn of world judgment in 11:17, for God's coming will then have become an eternal present. Precisely this same expression is met in the middle of the bowl visions (16:5), characterized by this twofold time formula as the beginning of God's eschatological inroad into history! And therefore the domain of these "last plagues" is extended over the whole world.

These final manifestations of the wrath of God in world history are marked out by two characteristics which clarify their purpose.

---

a connection between the three "woes" of the Revelation and the Mandaean book of John (M. Lidzbarski, *Das Johannesbuch der Mandäer* [1915], p. 236) seems to me, on account of the wholly diverse connections in the context, to be altogether accidental and far-fetched.

127 Reisner's allegorizing (*op. cit.*, pp. 76f.) on the Old Testament story shows at most how arbitrary all other interpretations are. With as much justification any sort of thing could be seen in the trumpets. There is no way to justify this manner of exegesis.

128 Cf. p. 110.

129 See G. Delling, *op. cit.*, pp. 125f.

Both features stand in the deepest connection with the primitive Christian schedule of time.

1) The bowl visions exhibit a striking similarity of form to the trumpet plagues. This similarity has been explained by most recent commentators[130] by the fact that chapters 15–16 were constructed in imitation of the trumpet plagues as an introduction to chapters 17–18.

Chapters 17–18 have been understood thereby as an originally independent fragment worked into the Revelation. This would imply a weakened imagination on the part of the Seer and suggest that he could no longer produce an original creation.[131] Spitta thinks in terms of a tradition similar to the trumpet visions (source J2) which the writer had lit upon as a late touch and worked a recapitulated form of into his book. However, positive support for this construction is lacking in the text, and it would offer no opportunity to explain the characteristic dissimilarities in the two series of visions. Nevertheless, all critical questions solve themselves on positive grounds if the intention of the Seer to portray only the last section of the intermediary time in chapters 15–16 is recognized.[132] The similarity of the two series is grounded in their essential homogeneity: The last section of the intermediary time brings no new factor into the picture of world history; its quality remains the same, although there enters in 2) an intensifying of the eschatological event: instead of the one third or one quarter, the *whole* earth, *all of mankind,* is now drawn into its compass.

From this historical-theological viewpoint is to be explained the intensifying of the sixth visions of the seal and trumpet series: the first five include the whole intermediary time, the sixth the last section of it which leads directly to the End. Thus chapters 15–16 portray nothing other than a broadened exposition of the sixth seal and the sixth trumpet.

The insertion of 16:5, intruded between the sixth and seventh bowls (after 16:16, cf. pp. 10f.), shows this same twofold precision.

---

130 For example, Völter, Erbes, Vischer, Weizsäcker, Bousset, Lohmeyer. Boismard assigns it to both his apocalypses.

131 Bousset, *Die Offenbarung Johannes, ad loc.*

132 It can thereby very well involve genuine visions. Cf. Ch. Brütsch, *Clarté de l'Apocalypse* (1955), pp. 164f.

It expresses nothing new, constituting only a repetition of the cry directed to the whole End time (3:3; 22:20), but yet it contains, here in the final days of world history, a special urgency and heightened meaning.[133]

O. Cullmann has characterized this ultimately final time (in the New Testament view) as a time which contains, "compressed so to speak in a specially concentrated manner in that moment," what has already happened in the intermediary time and, accordingly, "constitutes a unity with the whole occurrence of this intermediary time."[134]

The bowl vision closes again in the seventh vision, like the survey of the entire intermediary time, with a view of the End, the fall of Babylon. Chapters 15–16 thus act as an introduction to the scene in chapters 17–18.

The destruction of Babylon is the final act of judgment prior to the world judgment. This last section (17:1–19:10) brings a perceptive portrayal of the nature of Babylon, annexes a further survey of the whole intermediary time (*qua* Babylon and its beast), and concludes again with the breaking in of the kingdom of God (19:1-10[135]).

Therewith is closed off the first great section of time in the Revelation.

With this investigation we gain an insight into the understanding of the scheduling of time in John's Revelation. Although John thinks very closely along the lines of the Old Testament and later Jewish testimony, yet precisely at this point he diverges totally from them. For he recognizes in the historical Christ event the beginning of the End time confirmed by God himself.

While in the Jewish apocalyptic all history is directed toward the End[136] and moves on according to plan, John recognizes in the historical Christ event an eschatological event already occurred, he

133 This same distribution into final and ultimately final time is found also in Jewish and primitive Christian eschatologies: cf. 2 Esdras 5:2; Daniel 12:1 (Volz, *op. cit.*, pp. 153ff.), Matthew 24:21f.; Mark 13:19f. To this belongs the outlook according to which the Antichrist would first become manifest right at the end of the intermediary time.
134 Cullmann, *Christ and Time*, II, 4.
135 Cf. pp. 11f.
136 Cf. especially D. Rössler, *Gesetz und Geschichte* (1960), pp. 55f.

sees in Jesus the revelation of the meaning and goal of all history, and in the risen Lord, the lord of final history.

Two laws are interwoven in this End time: it shows a qualitative unity and a quantitative intensifying and broadening of its determinative elements pointing toward its End.[137]

The Revelation gives a portrayal of the End time in peculiar repetitions which deal with this period from various viewpoints. This peculiarity of style and thought of the Revelation calls to mind very strongly the Gospel of John and the Johannine letters. A principal characteristic of Johannine thought is the meditative thinking in great circles of ideas.[138] The Johannine writings tend to obscure clarity and transparency by their construction. It is especially so in 1 John, where the outline and forward movement of thought is not defined, as it is in the Gospel, by a historically qualified time-place scheme. But even in the Gospel the individual pericopes are not connected in a strictly logical manner; rather, each one contains the whole in itself, without a clear advance in thought. They concern themselves much more with parallel developments of the self-same theme. This stylistic peculiarity resembles a chain whose parts connect with one another and are bound indissolubly together, whose links, however, each constitute a compact, self-contained whole. This explains the frequent repetitions, which are not simply doublets, but reveal a view of the same fact from distinctive perspectives.[139] The Revelation's mode of thought is wholly similar, running to great circles and images, each of which over and over again displays a more or less compact train of thought. Therefore, neither recapitulation theories nor schemata which would understand the visions as successive, temporally distinct occurrences will

---

137 Something similar is shown by the "degenerative theory" in the four-kingdom arrangement of Daniel and the myths connected thereto. Cf. W. Baumgartner, "Zu den vier Reichen von Daniel 2," *ThZ* 1 (1945).

138 Cf. thereto especially W. von Loewenich, "Johanneisches Denken, ein Beitrag zur Erkenntnis der johanneischen Eigenart," *ThBl* 11 (1936), pp. 260–275; Max Pohlenz, "Der Prolog des Johannesevangeliums" (Appendix I, to the essay "Paulus und die Stoa"), *ZNW* 42 (1949), pp. 98–101, and F. Montagnini, *Riv. Bibl.* 5 (1957), pp. 180–187.

139 Cf. in the Gospel the various conceptions, "life, light, love, truth," which peculiarly intersect each other, are identical, and yet again are differentiated from one another, and which are held together and have their focal point in the "I am" (cf. Ed. Schweizer, *Ego eimi, FRL* [1939], especially pp. 122ff.).

This character of Johannine thought is especially evident in the chapter on the "Intention of the Evangelist" in O. Cullmann's *Early Christian Worship* (1953). Here the essential basis of this peculiarity is displayed.

satisfy the need to explain the remarkable interlacing and successiveness of the series of visions.[140] The uniformity of the visions, which are yet extended in a continuing movement of thought, lends itself very well for understanding on the basis of the character of Johannine thinking. The same peculiarity is shown by the piece inserted between the great vision cycles, and in which is contained again the whole intermediary time. The messages to the churches can be very well compared with the Prologue of John's Gospel. Even in the messages—as in John's Prologue—the movements and themes of the book are present embryonically.

With the Jewish and primitive Christian eschatology, the Revelation ties up—not formally but with regard to the contents at hand—its two-aeon teaching: the old earthly history stands over against the consummated world. With the Old Testament, Jewish, and primitive Christian outlook, the Revelation connects also the application of the category of time to the aeon before as well as to the aeon after the Parousia.[141]

3. THE LORD OF TIME

In the whole Revelation, God is the sovereign lord of creation and history.[142] This lordship explains above all the majestic and glorious scene of God and his court which introduces the whole history of the End time (4–5). Right at the beginning attention is directed to the throne, the embodiment and sign of God's lordship. And God's nature is described by a participial expression: the one being seated (4:3, etc.).[143] His lordship finds its expression also in the worship of the heavenly court, the twenty-four elders,[144] the four living creatures,[145] and all the other angels.

---

140 G. Bornkamm, "Die Komposition der apokalyptischen Visionen in der Johannes-Offenbarung," *ZNW* (1937), pp. 132–149, has worked out in a detailed fashion the similarities and differences. Yet it appears to me that this interpretation which Bornkamm gives for the peculiarity of the book does not correspond to the situation.

141 Thus also in the Jewish eschatology so far as it is not accompanied by Greek influence, as in Slavonic Enoch 65:7f. Cf. Bousset, *Die Religion des Judentums*, p. 244; Volz, *op. cit.*, p. 263; Sasse, *TWB* 1:202ff.

142 Cf. P. Fannon, "The Apocalypse," *Scripture* 26 (1962), pp. 33–43.

143 Of an earthly king, Exodus 12:29; 1 Kings 1:48; 8:25; transferred to God, Psalms 80:1; 99:1. God is the one "enthroned upon the cherubim"; see O. Schmitz, *TWB* 3:162, and G. Delling, *op. cit.*, pp. 122f.

144 The twenty-four elders can only be thought of as angelic beings, not as human—in spite of the arguments of A. Feuillet, "Les vingt-quatre vieillards de l'Apocalypse," *RB* (1958), pp. 5–32—for not only is the inclusion of individual godly persons in the

The time-referenced descriptions of God, *ho ōn kai ho ēn kai ho erchomenos*,[146] are of course quite meaningful for our context. The Seer is certainly dependent on Jewish traditions in his formulation,[147] although he has altered it in his characteristic manner. God is not only the one who ever exists, who lives in a temporal or supertemporal eternity, but who, in identity with his historical manifestations in past and present, "comes." The eschatological coming of God in the Parousia of Jesus is certainly the main point here (1:7; 3:11; 16:15; 22:7, 12, 17, 20), but perhaps also there is involved the present coming of the Lord for salvation or judgment (3:20; 2:5, 16).

Because the coming one is identical with the crucified (1:7f.), God's future will be the future of the Christ who has already appeared, who is the lord of the whole of created time, the lord of history, and who indeed as its founder (*ho prōtos*) and its redeemer died for the creation at the midpoint of time, who lives as the resurrected one (*ho zōn kai egenomēn nekros kai idou zōn eimi eis tous aiōnas tōn aiōnōn*), and who will come again as its fulfiller (*ho eschatos*), 1:17f.[148]

As lord of time, God (and Christ) establishes times and sea-

---

innermost circle of God's court most difficult to place in the scope of the Revelation's theology, but they also have duties which in the Revelation are appropriate only to angels: they interpret the events which are seen (5:5; 7:13–17), they mediate the prayers of the saints (5:8; cf. 8:3–5!), and they attend God's course from creation (4:10f.) through the central event of time in Christ's appearance (5:5, 9f.) and until the End (11:16–18; 19:4), and the Seer calls one of the elders *kyrios* (7:14). It cannot be said with certainty from whence the conception of these twenty-four heavenly elders comes; cf. H. Bietenhard, *Die himmlische Welt im Urchristentum und Spätjudentum* (1951), pp. 57–60. Special attention should be paid to Isaiah 24:23, where perhaps angels (adjacent to the host of heaven, the sun and moon) are also called elders.

145 The four living creatures are patterned after Ezekiel 1 and Isaiah 6:2; see H. Bietenhard, *op. cit.*, p. 62.

146 1:4, 8; 4:8. *Ho ēn* replaces the participle for past time. The formula is a translation and new explanation of the Old Testament name of Yahweh; cf. E. Schild, "I am that I am," *Vetus Testamentum* 4 (1954), pp. 296–307, and L. M. Pakozdy, "Die Deutung des Jahvenamens in Ex 3:14," *Judaica* 2 (1955), pp. 193–208.

147 From a later period we know the formula "I am who I was . . . I am now and I am in the future," Midrash of Exodus Rabba 3 (69c); cf. Jerusalem Targum (Pseudo-Jonathan); Deuteronomy 32:39; see Delling, *op. cit.*, pp. 126f.

148 "Alpha and Omega, Beginning and End, the First and the Last, are not formulas of a pantheistic or panentheistic belief about the cosmos, rather . . . an expression of faith in the omnipotent lord of history," H. D. Wendland, *Geschichtsanschauung und Geschichtsbewusstsein im Neuen Testament* (1938), p. 53. Cf. my article "Alpha" in the *Biblisch-Historischen Handwörterbuch* I (1962), p. 1. In 3:14 Christ is similarly termed "the beginning of God's creation" (cf. Prov. 8:22; 3:19; Ps. 136:5; Col. 1:18). Christ is thereby designated as the outer and inner ground of the creation.

sons.[149] Thus he defines the beginning of the End time longed for in the Old Testament and Judaism by the sending of his Son (12:5). The numbers in the Revelation also serve to express this mastery of time and its history by God and Christ (cf. the Danielic times in chapters 11–13, which delineate the time of the church and of the Antichrist; cf. also the statement in 9:5 and 2:21: *edōka chronon*). This thinking is also served, however, by the formal pattern of groups of seven, whose individual events are brought about by angels sent by God. The series of seven organize the End time according to the divine plan.[150] Thus the mathematically defined form of the book contains an eminently theological import.

God's lordship over time is illustrated also by the figures of the *biblion* and *biblaridion,* which characterize the End time as determined by God's plan of salvation. Christ alone as ruler of time and history can reveal to mankind this plan of salvation.[151] And in the same way this thought is served by the emphatic allusion to definite points of time within history which God has fixed (9:15). God's act defines also the very breaking in of the kingdom of God (19:11ff.).

It is also now to be understood from God's and Christ's absolute power of disposal over time that he can give mankind in their appointed time a portion in his decisive, historically unique act of redemption in the past and in the time of consummation as well:[152] they are already written in the book of life, already bought and purified through the blood of the Lamb; already having white garments, they are already kings and priests (cf. 1:6; 3:4; 5:10), and yet they still live in their particular time before the consummation. But this participation in the past and future in the Revelation (and in the rest of the New Testament) is not to be understood as indicating that God suspends for the believer time and its passage and therewith the special meaning of the actual portion of time in which the believer lives; nor that the believer has been removed from his association with history in order to become contemporary with the

---

149 Cf. 7:1; 9:13f.; 15:1, 7; 16:1; 14:15. Similarly in Jewish apocalypses, for example, Ethiopian Enoch 92:2: "The Holy One has appointed days for all things"; 2 Esdras 14:5, 11; Syriac Baruch 54:1; 69:2; Assumption of Moses 12:5.
150 Cf. the organization into groups of three and four.
151 5:5, 9f.
152 Lohmeyer has especially emphasized this, but he has explained it erroneously by his thesis about the "timelessness of the Revelation."

historical Christ event in such a way as to make past, present, and future interchangeable and insignificant for the believer,[153] nor yet in such a way that the Christ event might become an eschatological event of the present in that the event's significance has been understood "in the concrete fulfillment of the life of the believer."[154] Such an understanding would deprive the occurrence of the past of its once-for-all meaning as an actual salvation event. No, God's lordship over time is to be understood to mean that he who is distinguished by his redemptive act in the past becomes contemporary with the believer and permits the fruit of his redemptive transaction to become effectual in him, primarily as an anticipation of the consummation and only in partial realization, given by his Spirit (cf. III, 1 and 3).

153 Cf. Lohmeyer, *op. cit.*, p. 189.
154 Cf. Bultmann, *Kerygma and Myth* (1953), pp. 35–38.

III

The End Time

1. THE TIME OF CHRIST

The End time begins with the historical event of the first Parousia of Jesus Christ, which gives that time its character. Therefore we shall inquire first of all into the understanding of this historical Christ event in the Revelation.

A detailed description and interpretation is found in the twelfth chapter. We have already spoken of the overall conception of the chapter's three pericopes. Now we direct our attention to the representation of Christ. His appearing is described as his birth on earth. He is threatened by Satan, but not defeated. Instead, his elevation to the throne achieves for him a decisive victory over Satan, such that the angels under Michael's leadership can bring the dragon's hosts to destruction.[1] That Christ himself does not engage in battle with the dragon is significant in the context of the Revelation's christology. Nowhere does John mention such a battle (not even in the portrayal of the Parousia in 19:11ff.), for only as the Lamb who dies for the world does Christ win his battle (5:5, 9; 3:21).[2] And thus, according to the interpretive hymn of 12:10-12, mankind's possibility of victory over the dragon is found only "by the blood of the Lamb," that is, in the death of Jesus for them and therefore only "by the word of their testimony," whose content is the victory promised them by the Lamb's death!

---

1 Charles Brütsch, *op. cit.*, p. 135, rightly calls the angels' battle "a clean-up operation"!

2 *Sōtēria* has, in the hymn of 12:10 as well as in 7:10 and 19:1, an Old Testament ring: "an act of divine salvation" in the sense of "victory" (cf. Pss. 80:2; 74:12ff., and above all Deut. 33:29; Zeph. 3:17); see R. H. Charles, *op. cit.*, Vol. 1, p. 211; G. Fohrer, *TWB* 7:976, and W. Foerster, *TWB* 7:999.

The Christ event, the coming of Christ to earth, his death for salvation, and his victory through the ascension, all lead to the conclusion that now the time introduced by the Christ event and ruled over by Christ is characterized as the messianic time. Conceptions from out of Judaism are thereby taken over and transformed. Judaism thought of the messianic kingdom either as identical with the consummated time of salvation or again as a period prior to the general time of consummation, a period of national salvation.[3] In the Revelation, a Christian view is developed which is parallel to a certain degree to the second, late form of the Jewish hope. This view understands the time between the first appearance of Christ on earth and the End event as an anticipatory, especially messianic, period of salvation history. But any nationalistic association is lacking.[4]

As does the Jewish messianic time, the Christian End time of the Revelation (and of the rest of the New Testament) offers now a share in the blessings of eschatological salvation: The Messiah is present in the church,[5] especially in the messianic banquet.[6] The now-present Messiah gives his companions in salvation a portion in the eschatological redemption, in that he, through his sufferings, fulfills for them their hope for forgiveness of sins[7] (1:5[8]).

The main representation, in which Christ is ever and again seen as the lord of the intermediary time, is the Lamb who was slain. This marks him out as the Messiah who has become the redeemer through his sacrificial death.

Also, the traditional figure of the "Son of Man,"[9] which the Revelation uses not only in a futuristic sense (14:14) but also for the lord of the intermediary time (1:12ff.), gets its stamp from the suffering of the redeemer (1:18). That in both the traditional expression is used in the eschatological sense is shown by the circum-

---

3 Cf. Volz, *op. cit.*, pp. 63ff., and Strack and Billerbeck, *op. cit.*, III:824ff.
4 The transformation is grounded fundamentally and—as we shall see—centrally in the Christian faith.
5 14:1–5.
6 3:20.
7 Cf. Psalms of Solomon 17; Testament of Levi 18; Similitudes of Enoch; 2 Esdras 13:26; Targum of Isaiah 53:4, 6, 12; Volz, *op. cit.*, p. 221.
8 The reading *lousanti hēmas apo* . . . is really synonymous; cf. 7:14; 5:9; 14:3; 22:14.
9 John retains here the Old Testament wording and does not use the concept as a title; cf. T. Holtz, *op. cit.*, pp. 116–128.

stance that the Revelation in 14:14 uses the Danielic conception in its originally futuristic meaning.[10] Contrasting with Daniel 7, there enters here a characteristic expansion which transforms the traditional figure into something new. The robe is particularly mentioned, which, with its girdle up about the breast, recalls the robe of the high priest.[11] The image is certainly also influenced by Daniel 10:5f.[12] And add to this the significant association of elements taken from the figure of the "Ancient of Days," which is effected in 1:14.[13] This association expresses clearly the real homogeneity of the Son of Man with God and transfers to him the attributes of the divine judge of the world. As world judge characterizes the Son of Man, so also does the sword which issues from his mouth (1:16a).[14] This transference of the office of world judge to the royal-priestly Son of Man[15] shows again how consciously the Seer here understands the image of the Son of Man in its eschatological significance. In this way he designates the time since the historical act of redemption (1:18) as eschatological-messianic. Therein the specifically Christian view of the intermediary time expresses itself: the End event has already begun, but it is first consummated when this same Son of Man comes again in the

---

10 Also, for Daniel the Son of Man, as the personal embodiment of the people of God, is the one who leads to eschatological salvation (Dan. 7:27), and against whom the four beasts, i.e., kings, as embodiments of the kingdoms, stand (cf. Volz, *op. cit.,* pp. 128, 186–190; W. Bousset, *op. cit.,* p. 267; J. Jeremias, *Jesus als Weltvollender, BFTh* [1930], pp. 53–57). The obviously clear dependence on Daniel speaks against Boll's derivation (*op. cit.,* p. 50).

11 Cf. thereto J. Gnilka, "Die Erwartung des messianischen Hohenpriesters in den Schriften von Qumran und im Neuen Testament," *Revue de Qumran* 2 (1960), pp. 395–426; T. Holtz, *op. cit.,* pp. 118–121; J. Jeremias, *Jerusalem zur Zeit Jesu* (1958), Part II, pp. 3f.

12 Cf. the "eyes like flaming torches" of Daniel 10:6.

13 One is struck yet again by the freedom of conception which eloquently testifies that the Revelation is no literary compilation of traditional materials, but is made up of original visionary imagery (with traditional materials which match their prototypes not merely formally but materially as well).

14 The conception of Isaiah 11:4 is united, with its concept of the word of judgment, to the two-edged sword (cf. Isa. 49:2; Ps. 149:6; Ps. of Sol. 17:24, 35; Wisdom of Sol. 18:15; Heb. 4:12; Eph. 6:17) and transferred to the Son of Man (cf. especially Ad. Schlatter, *op. cit.,* p. 37). Sebastian Bartina's conjecture that the sword is thought of as coming not out of the mouth, but out of the neck of the robe, is unsatisfactory, for the Old Testament has previously made the association with the word essential; see "Una espada salía de la boca de su vestido," *Estudios Biblicos* 20:2 (1961), pp. 207–217.

15 Cf. Matthew 25:31ff.; Acts 10:42; 2 Corinthians 5:10. On the development of the "judge" idea, cf. Bousset, *Kyrios Christos, FRL,* 4th ed. (1935), p. 15, and R. Scott, "Behold, He Cometh with Clouds," *NTS* 5 (1959), pp. 127–132.

future (significantly, the "clouds" of the Parousia occur in 14:14, as well as in 1:7).

This eschatological Son of Man is, in the intermediary time, the now-present Messiah for his congregation, which is seen as in a vision in the figure of the seven lamps (1:20). The presence of Christ is also portrayed in the representation of the Lamb with the 144,000 on Zion (14:1-5).

The real presence in the intermediary time is only visionary, in pictorial form, not directly physical, as in the time of the historical Christ event. Joh. Weiss was completely right when he emphasized the distance of the figure of the Son of Man from the "remembered figure of the Jesus of the Gospels."[16] This, though, says nothing against the apostolicity of the author; rather, it is based on the fact that since the ascension Christ Jesus is no longer really visible to human eyes. Now only in visionary images, without historically personal features, can men be assured of his invisible presence.[17] This view characterizes the whole of primitive Christian literature without exception. The presence of Christ in the intermediary time is the presence of the Holy Spirit. The fact that the words of Jesus are identified with those of the Spirit points to this same thing (cf. the beginnings and closings of the letters to the churches, 2:1, 7, etc.).

It is a peculiarity of the Revelation that it can speak of the Spirit in the singular (2:7, 11, etc.; 14:13; 19:10; 22:17), and also as a group of seven (1:4; 3:1; 4:5f.; 5:6).[18]

That even the seven spirits are nothing else than the one Spirit of God is certain from 1:4, where grace and peace, gifts which God alone can give, are awaited from "him who is and who was and who is to come," the seven spirits, and Jesus Christ.[19] There is no reason to understand the other passages which speak of the seven

---

16 Joh. Weiss, *op. cit.*, pp. 609f.

17 Mk. Barth, *Der Augenzeuge* (1946), pp. 105f., 159, compares the Christ images of the Revelation to the Easter appearances of Jesus. The author of the Revelation raises no claim for such a comparison.

18 1:4 is no gloss. Lohmeyer's objections on metric and stylistic grounds are too subjective. Nor will it do to object that chapter 4 is "anticipated" by the verse, for the concern of 3:1 and 4:5 is the Holy Spirit, not angels (observe the diversity of words and symbols, which must not be obliterated, for it is consciously fixed in the Revelation). Cf. Strack and Billerbeck, *op. cit.*, III:788.

19 On the mediatory position of the Spirit, cf. 1 Peter 1:2; 2 Thessalonians 2:13f.

spirits as a known quantity in any other way. This conception of
the Spirit is moreover not wholly strange to the New Testament.
Paul can "individualize" the spirit which each individual has
received.[20]

The first mention of the seven spirits refers at once by the attri-
bute *enōpion tou thronou autou* to the figure of the spirits in 4:5.
Here the Spirit of God is shown in the figure of the seven burning
"torches of fire," which stand "in the space between the throne
and the elders."[21] It is in itself possible that the Jewish conception
of the seven angels of the throne has influenced the formation of
this image,[22] although it is to be observed that the function of the
spirits has nothing whatever in common with that of the Jewish
throne angels.[23] And the number seven, which characterizes the
whole book, is rather taken from the "full number" of the seven
churches, each of whom has "the Spirit" and whose fullness is described by the number seven.[24] Obviously, spirit and angel stand
near each other in the Revelation, for the angels are understood as
the working of God himself in creaturely disguise as in the Old
Testament, and yet the spirit—even in the form of the seven spirits
—is clearly distinguished from the angels, so that God and Christ
are not made one with the angels.[25]

---

20 1 Corinthians 14:14, and even Romans 1:9. To have the Spirit of Christ or to bear
Christ in oneself is all the same thing (Rom. 8·9, 10). Cf. W. G. Kümmel, *Römer 7
und die Bekehrung des Apostels Paulus* (1929), pp. 32f.; Ed. Schweizer, "Die 7 Geister
in der Apk.," *Ev. Theol.* 11 (1951–52), pp. 502–512; *TWB* 6:413ff.; K. II. Rengstorf,
TWB 2:623–631.

21 E. Lohmeyer, *op. cit., ad loc.*

22 So Ed. Schweizer, *op. cit.,* pp. 509–511, who identifies the seven spirits with God's
Spirit and with the throne angels as well and understands them to be figures parallel
to the angels of the churches. He sees in this the after-effect of the Jewish identification
of angels and spirits (especially in the literature of Qumran).

23 The formula *enōpion tou thronou autou* does not in any way identify the spirits
with the angels "as servants of God" (as P. Joüon, "Apocalypse 1:4," *Recherches de
Science Religieuse* 21 [1931], p. 487, supposes), for the formula in 4:5 is a purely
neutral definition of location which is repeated in 4:6 in connection with the portrayal
of the sea of glass. In late Judaism the concepts of angel and spirit could indeed be
interchanged, but it is doubtful whether they are identified with God's Spirit. "The
Spirit is no angelic heavenly being," nor is it to be identified with the intercessory
angels. See E. Sjöberg, *TWB* 6:385f., 387.

24 On the origin of the number seven as a holy number and an expression of fullness,
totality, cf. W. Rordorf, *op. cit.,* pp. 20–26; H. K. Rengstorf, *TWB* 2:623ff.; on the
number seven in the Old Testament, A. Haag, "Erwägungen über Beer-Seba," *Sacra
Pagina, Bibliotheca Ephemeridum Theologicarum Lovaniensium,* Vol. XII, XIII, Part 1,
pp. 335–345.

25 The "angels who stand before God" appear in 8:2ff. (wording different from
4:5!). The seven spirits are distinguished from the angels of the churches (1:20), and

The Apocalypse of Baruch 21:6 or the seven planets-fire altars of Mithras could be compared for the type of representational form,[26] yet Lohmeyer has already drawn attention in his commentary to the inadequacy of these parallels and therefore ascribes at least the meaning of the passage to the Seer. Another association seems to me to lie nearer at hand. In Acts 2:3 the Holy Spirit is associated with fire. And in the Old Testament there appears a striking correspondence to the conception of our book: in Genesis 15:17 Abraham experiences a theophany in which Yahweh reveals himself in two symbols: "behold, a smoking fire pot and a flaming torch."[27] Here the second expression, "a flaming torch," interests us. The LXX translates this with the plural *lampades pyros*. It seems to me thoroughly plausible to see a connection between Revelation 4:5 and the conceptions lying behind Genesis 15:17. So here also the torch's fiery sign is to be related to the Holy Spirit as best corresponding to the circumstances.

But the Spirit of God is also explained as the seven eyes with which the Lamb of God scans the earth. As he does so frequently, John recalls here the Old Testament, Zechariah 4:10:[28] "These seven are the eyes of the LORD, which range through the whole earth." We meet a similar conception in 2 Chronicles 16:9: "For the eyes of the LORD run to and fro throughout the whole earth." The seven eyes of God, which express God's all-inclusive vision,[29] and from which nothing remains hidden, are also possessed by the Lamb. John depends on the wording of Zechariah 4:10 and uses his own adaptation to give the meaning: *apestalmenoi eis pasan tēn gēn*.[30] For the Spirit creates understanding (cf. 1 Cor. 2), thus there is given the representation of the eyes as the organ of understanding.

---

according to 3:1 even belong to Christ as do the angels of the churches, but are individual creatures. The angel is not only the concrete form of the spirit (Ed. Schweizer, *op. cit.*, p. 510), not only the representative of the church before God, but is at the same time the form and representative of God in relation to the church and the world.

26 Cf. W. Bousset, *Die Offenbarung Johannes, ad loc.*

27 See H. Gunkel, *Genesis, Göttinger Handkommentar zum AT*, I, Vol. 1, 5th ed. (1922), pp. 181f.

28 Cf. Zechariah 3:9. On the problem of both passages, see L. G. Rignell, *Die Nachtgesichte des Sacharje, Eine exegetische Studie* (1950), pp. 130–134, 160–165.

29 See also Proverbs 15:3. The eyes of God as a representation of the divine vigilance and solicitude: 1 Kings 8:29; Deuteronomy 11:12; Psalms 33:18; 34:16.

30 The expression has nothing to do with the sending out of angels.

This divine Pneuma also gives to mankind insight into God's plan of salvation (1:10 and frequently), and brings about prophecy as Jesus' own testimony (19:10). Any insight which is termed *pneumatikōs* can hence be understood only as a Spirit-produced, prophetic insight.[31]

Thus, in the Spirit-presence of Christ during the intermediary time, the peculiar tension of this time becomes visible: it is the eschatological time of the Christ-presence; and yet, the full revelation and appearance of the Lord is still to come.

The same understanding of the intermediary time as the time of Christ is contained also in Revelation 1:10. Undoubtedly the "Lord's day" is indissolubly bound up with the resurrection of Jesus and his presence in the church.[32] The resurrection is an eschatological event.[33] The church of Jesus experiences even now the ardently awaited coming of the eschatological lord in the midst of a world which unsuspectingly and blindly passes him by. In Revelation 1:10 the characteristic time understanding of primitive Christianity is attested with special emphasis: the decisive new era has now arrived, all that remains is for the course of history to arrive at its final goal.

What we designate as End time or intermediary time between the Parousias of Jesus is thus the messianic time, the time of the veiled messianic kingdom. Its true nature is perceived only by a faith illuminated by the Holy Spirit. In this messianic time, Christ is already lord of the world, not of the church alone. We have recognized this as a basic conviction of the Revelation in chapter 5, where the opening of the scroll is entrusted to the Lamb. Christ is as the Lion of Judah, the ruler "to whom shall be the obedience of the peoples" (Gen. 49:10), the one who has received "authority" with his ascension (12:10). He is "Lord of lords and King of kings"

---

31 Ed. Schweizer, *TWB* 6:448: "in prophetic speech." Jerusalem is "examined with prophetic eyes."

32 Cf. W. Rordorf, *op. cit.*, pp. 216–233. There is perhaps associated with the term an allusion to the Last Day, with which the resurrection begins: "for the rest on the seventh day is the sign of the resurrection in the coming age," Vita Adae 51.

33 Cf. 1 Corinthians 15:23ff., where Paul includes the last phase of history since the historical Christ event until the Parousia in the eschatological resurrection epoch. And in Acts 2 the intermediary time is designated as the time of the beginning of the great day of God of Joel 2.

(17:14). In the same way in 1:5, Christ's saving significance for his church is coupled with his universal significance for world history: he is "the ruler of kings on earth."

The lordship of God and of Christ is effected again and again through the medium of supernatural beings: it is a lordship over the church (1:16; 2–3; 7:2; 8:3; 12:7ff.; 14:4) as well as over the world (6:1ff.; 7:1ff.; 8:2ff.; 9:14f.; 14:15, 17ff.; 15:1ff.; 19:17; 20:1). Often the orders of God and of Christ are transmitted to others by angelic beings, as in 6:1-8: the four "living creatures"[34] intervene actively in the structuring of world history (cf. also 15:7).[35] The Revelation knows—as does Judaism—a whole hierarchy of angelic beings with specific functions.[36]

2. THE TIME OF THE ANTICHRIST

It is inherent in the tension-filled nature of the End time that in it the victory of the Lord of history remains unquestioned while at the same time the powers of evil retain their active potentiality. Out of this antithesis there develops the dynamic and problematic quality of the national and salvation history of the End period. Whether thus the superiority of Christ and the irrevocable, once-for-all alteration of the nature of world history through the death and exaltation of Christ are taken wholly seriously, John must report the last, desperate effort of the adversaries in order to be able to interpret the whole depth of historical reality.

The Revelation sets forth the Old Testament and Jewish understanding of the powers at enmity with God, but shapes its representation in a thoroughly new manner. The basic conception is accompanied by the idea of the imitation and perversion of the divine nature.[37] Thus the evil power becomes real, corresponding to the threefold revelation of God (1:4) in a threefold form, as the dragon, the Antichrist, and the false prophet (12–13). The interest of the Seer, moreover, does not lie in the portrayal of their nature and their

---

34 They appear to be four of the highest angelic beings—whatever the Seer has seen concretely in them.

35 The figures have completely lost their astral origin, their task is not to bear God's throne (Gunkel, *Zum religionsgeschichtliches Verständnis des NT*, pp. 43ff.).

36 See Bousset, *Die Religion des Judentums*, Index, *s.v.* Engel.

37 Cf. especially E. Stauffer, *New Testament Theology* (1955), pp. 64–68.

kingdom; they come into view only insofar as they enter into the activity of history, that is, when the salvation events of God and Christ are involved.

John sees the chief of the spiritual powers at enmity with God in the figure of the dragon, who is explained as the ancient major opponent of God out of the Old Testament: the ancient serpent (12:9; cf. Gen. 3:1; Isa. 27:1), the devil and Satan, called the "accuser" (12:10; cf. Job 1:6ff.; 2:1ff.; Zech. 3:1), the "deceiver" (12:9; cf. 1 Chron. 21:1). The details of the dragon vision are easily understood. The red color emphasizes the stirring up of anxiety,[38] heads and horns are Old Testament expressions for power (Ps. 74:14, 1 Sam. 2:1 [R.S.V., "strength"], and frequently), as is the diadem (the beasts in Dan. 7 bear many heads and horns). The dragon would plunge the world into dark chaos (12:4a), but the satanic authority is made powerless (12:5ff.), so that the angels could cast him with his hosts out of heaven. This eschatological victory is put forth from a wholly Christian viewpoint: the destruction of Satan's power is quite irreversible, but its consequences are initially comprehensible only to the believers (12:10-12), not to the rest of the world.[39] His downfall is not quite his final removal, and he will exploit his last times on earth (12:12).[40] The rest of the New Testament agrees with the Revelation's representation of the significance of the historical Christ event. "The oldest conception, which arises in apostolic times, tells the story of Jesus under the sign of the battle with the devil and his hosts."[41]

---

38 Cf. my article "The Rider on the White Horse," *Interpretation* 18 (1964), pp. 407–418.

39 The Gospel of John proclaims the same thought in many variations (cf. John 3:18).

40 Cf. the age-old myth in Slavonic Enoch 29:4f. of the downfall of the devil in the air, which may well stand behind Ephesians 2:2. Naturally, one cannot speak here of "Satan becoming temporal," with H. Schlier, "Vom Antichrist," *Theologische Aufsätze K. Barth zum 50. Geburtstag* (1936), p. 117, nor of a "destruction of Satan's power as he enters temporality" (*op. cit.*, p. 113). Satan is and remains as a creature, associated from the beginning with temporality, for he certainly has no share in God's nature. Cf. the article by K. L. Schmidt, "Lucifer als gefallene Engelmacht," *Akademischer Vortrag in der Universität Basel, ThZ* 3 (1951), pp. 161–177.

41 W. Heitmüller, *Im Namen Jesu, FRL* (1903), p. 306 (cf. Matt. 12:29; Luke 10:18; Mark 1:39; 3:14; Testament of Levi 18; Testament of Simeon 6; Testament of Zebulun 9; Assumption of Moses 10:1ff.; Ginza 373). Cf. J. Jeremias, *Jesus als Weltvollender,* pp. 58–60; O. Bauernfeind, *Die Worte der Dämonen im Markusevangelium* (1927); J. M. Robinson, *The Problem of History in Mark* (1957), pp. 43–67.

The final epoch, the intermediary time, is distinguished by especially violent activity on the part of the satanic power (12:12). The intensifying of Satan's battle against God takes the form of his sending out two "beasts"[42] who are his creatures (13:2, 11). The first beast is unquestionably the Antichrist.[43] He is represented as the consummate opponent of Christ. The relation of the figure to Daniel 7 is most interesting. The number 3½ stems from Daniel. But while in Daniel the 3½ times designates only the final period prior to the End, in the Revelation the number has become a symbol of the whole End time and correspondingly the characters of the first three beasts of Daniel 7:4-6 have been concentrated into one.[44] In him, as the one sent by Satan, all the devilish powers of the End time are at work together. The mouth which slanders God (Dan. 7:8, 11, 25) also belongs to the elements which stem from Daniel, as does the aim of the beast: to make "war with the saints" (Dan. 7:21).

The apocalyptist now brings into view, with help throughout from traditional images, a new reality. Its figure is fully stamped by thought about the Antichrist, formed by believers' knowledge about the historical form of the Christ revelation in Jesus.[45]

As Christ wears many diadems (19:12), so the Antichrist wears ten, and as Christ bears a name (19:12, 13, 16), so the Antichrist bears the "blasphemous name."[46] As God gives over to his Son a throne and lordship (12:5; 3:21), so the dragon gives to the beast his power and his throne and his great authority (13:2, 13). As

---

42 *Estathē* is the original reading; cf. J. Schmid, "Zur Textkritik der Apk.," *ZNW* 43 (1950/51), p. 125.

43 *Antichristos* first appears in the later Christian literature, in the New Testament only in 1 and 2 John (Cf. W. Bousset, *Der Antichrist*, pp. 86–88).

44 "The sea" (Dan. 7:3) is in Revelation 13:1 representative of the abyss, the place of the demons and the damned, for the demonic figures (11:7; 17:8) come forth from there. Also, in Revelation 20:13, the sea becomes meaningfully understandable only in terms of Hades and Thanatos (cf. my article, *op. cit.*, p. 410). The earthly sea according to ancient tradition is the image of the gloomy underworld and therefore no longer present in the new world (21:1); cf. Philippe Reymond, *L'Eau, sa vie, et sa signification dans l'ancien testament* (1958), pp. 212–214.

45 Cf. my article "Antichrist" in the *Biblisch-Historischen Handwörterbuch* I (1962), pp. 97f., and the literature mentioned there.

46 Blasphemy belongs to the central expressions of the Antichrist theme and in the Revelation has nothing to do with the Roman caesar-cult, much more with the judaizing and syncretistic heresies: 2:2, 9, 13ff., 20ff.; 3:9, 17. Blasphemy of God's name is traditional: Daniel 8:10; Sibylline Oracles 5:33ff.; Ascension of Isaiah 4:6. Wholly in this context also stands the traditional "who is like the beast?" (Exod. 15:11). Sibylline Oracles 3:75, 352; 2 Esdras 8:15.

Christ "ransoms" men and leads them to God (5:9; 14:4), so the Antichrist misleads men to worship of the dragon (13:4).[47] As Christ is the victor and lord of the world (5:5), so also is victory and lordship given to the Antichrist (13:7). Christ and Antichrist make definitive proclamations of both their victories in the death of the martyrs (12:11; 13:7). And even the most essential distinguishing mark of the beast serves this antithesis. It is the fatal wound which is healed (13:3, repeated as a special mark of wonderment in 13:12, 14!).

Most interpreters assume that John had appropriated here the Nero myth and make use of this notion then as an argument for the political interpretation of the whole chapter. I believe that this thesis will not hold up under close scrutiny. The form of the Nero myth in which Nero has not died but fled to the Parthians is not involved here, for the death of the beast is spoken of. The other form speaks of Nero's return from the underworld.[48] But even of that we hear nothing here, only of the healing of the fatal wound. If now by the beast the Roman empire were meant and by the heads, the emperors, this would yield a statement which no author in the first century would be capable of. For not for Romans, Jews, or Christians was the suicide of Nero a threat to the Roman empire and his return from the underworld a reawakening! But the cutting off of one head leads to the death of the whole beast (13:14).[49]

Then add to this that the beast is active without interruption during the entire End time, which, as we have seen, began with the historical Christ event according to John's view (13:5).[50] There is lacking the slightest allusion to any potential historical interpretation in the entire scene, in contrast to chapter 17, where historical situations are directly spoken of and where, strikingly, there is lacking precisely the central distinctive mark of the beast in chapter 13,

---

47 The whole godless world falls under the satanic authority. *Hoi katoikountes epi tēs gēs* becomes a collective term for the godless (cf. 2 Esdras 3:34f.; 4:39; 7:72; Apoc. Bar. 48:32, 40, etc.).

48 Cf. on the whole problem: Tacitus, *Hist.* 2:8; Suetonius, *De vita Caesarum* (Nero), 6:57; Sibylline Oracles 4:119ff., 137f.; Ascension of Isaiah 4:2.

49 This is properly emphasized by P. S. Minear in his much too little noticed article, "The Wounded Beast," *JBL* 72 (1953), pp. 93–101. "His death did not jeopardize the power of the empire, because he died as a fugitive and enemy of the state" (p. 97). Cf. also the difficulties which Charles, *op. cit.*, p. 350, is aware of.

50 The passive *edothē* paraphrases God's action.

the sword wound which leads to death, and where a time is spoken of during which the beast is not on the earth (17:8).[51]

The death and resuscitation of the beast is moreover better explained without difficulties as central references in the context of the "imitation motifs" within the Antichrist theme. They are understood as counterparts to the death and resurrection of Jesus. This is shown in the taking up of the same terminology (13:3, *hōs esphagmenēn;* 5:6, *arnion hōs esphagmenon*). *Sphazein* in other respects simply forbids thinking of Nero's suicide, but rather of a blow from an enemy's hand.[52] Who delivers the blow is not mentioned and is unimportant, for the intention of the Seer is simply to present "the beast" as the consummate opponent of Christ Jesus, as the Antichrist.

The intention of the Antichrist becomes openly visible in his battle against the church of Jesus (13:7). For this he makes use of his helper, the false prophet (13:11ff.; 16:13), who belongs inseparably to the first beast and to the dragon. The conception of the two monsters who will reveal themselves at the end of time is also alive in apocalyptic Judaism: ". . . thereupon the Messiah will begin to reveal himself. And Behemoth will reveal himself from his land and Leviathan will arise out of the sea" (Syr. Bar. 29:3f.). But the two are not specifically Antichrist figures. In the Revelation the mythical materials undergo a complete alteration, occasioned by the new historical revelation of God in Jesus Christ.

The triadic conception invites in the second beast a diabolical mimicry of God's Spirit. And actually his name intimates this: as a "false prophet" (19:20) he is the instrument of the revelation of the satanic authority, as the Holy Spirit is the mediator of God's revelation (2:7, etc.; 14:13; 19:10).[53] Again all the details of the

---

51 How a consciously historical interpretation of mythical material appears, we learn in Sibylline Oracles 4:119ff., 137f.; Ascension of Isaiah 4:2: ". . . Beliar . . . has come down out of his firmament in the form of a man, . . . a mother-killer . . ."

52 Minear would therefore think even of the sword of Christ (1:16; 2:12, 16; 19:15, 21) in consideration of the fact that *plēgē* in the Revelation always means the divine judgment (*op. cit.,* pp. 98f.). But John does not give this interpretation; just as little does he give Minear's interpretation of the resuscitation: "The continued life of the mortally wounded beast depends upon the worship which men give to it" (p. 99).

53 1 John 4:1–3 also speaks quite similarly of a "spirit" or of many "spirits" of the Antichrist, who are at work behind and in human false prophets. *Pneuma* in 1 John 4 is not identical with "teacher" (R. Bultmann, *Das Johannesevangelium, Kritisch-*

vision serve this counterpart thought. As the Lamb bears horns (5:6), so the second beast bears two horns "like a lamb." *Agnum fingit ut agnum invadat* (Primasius). But his speech betrays his nature, he speaks "like a dragon" (13:11).[54]

In contrast to the Holy Spirit, who leads men to the worship of God, is the office of the false spirit, who misleads men to the worship of the Antichrist (13:12). In order to accomplish his deception he executes "signs," which are of course to be understood as perversions of the miracles of Jesus.[55] The fire miracle calls to mind the forerunner of the messiah, Elijah. But the whole picture is however conceived in so specifically a Christian manner that the closest explanation appears to be that the fire should be taken as an imitation and perversion of the Pentecostal wonders of the Holy Spirit.[56] For in Acts 2:17ff. (cf. also Acts 2:3) fire is also connected with the wonders of Pentecost. It is also striking that the Apocalypse of Elijah cites the same passage from Joel as Acts does in connection with the miracles of the Antichrist.

The chief act of the false spirit consists in his leading men to make an image of the Antichrist and in his making it live. Even this is a traditional detail.[57] Here, however, it constitutes not only a coordinated element, but stands in the center and contains a remarkable absolutizing as *the act* of the false spirit. One is likely here to think in terms of an embodiment of a heathen priesthood or of some individual cult such as the cult of caesar.[58] But the statements of the Revelation are much too general to allow any reference to

---

exegetischer Kommentar über das NT, ed. H. A. W. Meyer, 11th ed. [1950], pp. 98f.); it carries its proper superhuman sense and is to be distinguished from the false prophet himself (cf. H. Windisch, *Erster und Zweiter Johannesbrief, Hdb. L.,* Vol. 15, 2nd ed. [1930], on 1 John 4, *ad loc.*).

54 Figure and voice characterize a person according to his "external and internal qualities" (cf. Lohmeyer's examples, *op. cit.,* p. 113: John 5:37; 20:14ff.; Ginza 154, 181, and Bultmann, *ibid.,* p. 200, footnote 6).

55 The detail is traditional; cf. Mark 13:22 and parallels; 2 Thessalonians 2:9f.; 2 Esdras 5:4; Ascension of Isaiah 4:5ff.; Apocalypse of Elijah (G. Steindorff, *Die Apokalypse des Elias, eine unbekannte Apokalypse und Bruchstücke der Sophoniasapokalypse, TU,* Vol. 2, Part 30 [1899], p. 161); Sibylline Oracles 3:66ff.; Didache 16:4. The Mandaean literature specifically speaks of both signs and wonders of the false messiah (Ginza 29 of fire miracles). Further examples are given by M. Dibelius, *Thessalonicher I. II./ Philipper, Hdb. L.,* Vol. 11, 3rd ed. (1937), on 2 Thessalonians 2:9.

56 So also E. Reisner, *op. cit., ad loc.*

57 Ascension of Isaiah 4:11; cf. Dibelius, *op. cit.,* on 2 Thessalonians 2:5. Talking idols are known in antiquity.

58 See the enumeration in Brütsch, *op. cit.,* p. 145. P. Touilleux, *L'Apocalypse et les cultes de Domitien et de Cybele* (1935), suggests the cult of Cybele.

any specific cult. The false prophet is to be understood as completely parallel to the Antichrist as a superhistorical satanic person. With the presentation of this image in which deity manifests itself as a "living incarnation,"[59] the Seer describes the origin of all religion:[60] mankind makes itself an image (presumably of the redeemer, in reality however) of the beast, the false redeemer from hell. Thus all religion, all false conceptions of God, are stigmatized as idolatrous representations of the Antichrist (cf. Exod. 20:4 LXX: *ou poiēseis seautō eidōlon*). The antichristlike spiritual power causes the image to speak, that is, the image becomes for men an objective source of revelation.[61] As giver of "breath" (13:15), the false prophet is again the satanic counterpart of the Holy Spirit, who is termed in Revelation 11:11 "breath of life" (cf. John 6:63).

Just as God's own people bear a seal (7:1ff.), so the people of the beast bear a sign which is indeed suitable in designating the opposition of mankind itself to God's sign (13:16). Men give themselves a sign of their unity—who does not associate himself with them will be excluded from the possibility of making a living (13:16f.). A prime example of this religious fanaticism, to which Antipas fell victim, is reported from Pergamum by Revelation 2:14. The city was renowned for its cultic buildings, above all for its gigantic altar to Zeus-Soter, although as much for the temple to Asclepius which made the city the "Lourdes of antiquity."[62] Hence, it is not surprising that "Satan's throne" is seen in Pergamum (2:13) and that the chief danger of the seven churches in Asia Minor lay in syncretistic worship.[63] Neither the letters to the seven churches (2–3) nor chapters 12–13 have anything to do with the cult of caesar, which played no major role in Asia Minor at that time.

We see thus that in Revelation 12–13 the image of the satanic

---

59 Boman, *op. cit.*, p. 94.

60 Brütsch has properly observed the several instances of the verb *poiein* in 13:12. "This excessive activism is typical of those who do not live by grace" (*op. cit.*, p. 145).

61 Testimonies to such an evaluation of heathen religiosity are found, for instance, in LXX Deuteronomy 32:17; Jubilees 11:3f.; 19:28; Ethiopian Enoch 19:1.

62 Joh. Weiss, *op. cit., ad loc.*; cf. Th. Zahn, *op. cit.*, pp. 255ff.; R. Reitzenstein, *Die Vorgeschichte der christlichen Taufe* (1929), p. 207. To Asclepius was also attributed the power to awake the dead, Justin, *Dialogus* 69:3.

63 P. Janzon, "Nikolaiterna i Nya Testamentet och i fornkyrkan," *Svensk Exegetisk Arsbok* 21 (1956), pp. 82–108. He shows that the problem lay not in gnosticism but in local syncretism.

powers which stand behind the history of the intermediary time is formed out of specifically Christian thought: Satan, imitating God, sends out his Antichrist and his Antispirit.[64] Nowhere else in the New Testament is the image of the satanic powers maintained in such minuteness of detail and inner compactness. But in fact, this same understanding is not found here only. The real roots of this Christian conception of the Antichrist lie not only in Judaism—although the Old Testament and Judaism naturally prepared the way for this view of history—but also and quite particularly in the historical Christ event. It can be said yet more specifically of the role of the Antichrist as Volz[65] has done in the case of the role of the devil: the conception was first formed on the basis of "the person of the Savior." Its presentation is wholly tied to the historical Christ-figure of Jesus by the law of contrariety. The Antichrist is "another" (John 5:43) who comes "in his own name," in his own authority.[66]

The functioning of the Antichrist follows simultaneously with or in direct connection to that of Christ on earth. The time of the Antichrist is the entire intermediary time (13:5)[67] and thus begins simultaneously with the hidden messianic kingdom and ends with it (19:19-21[68]). A New Testament parallel to this understanding of the intermediary time is found in the enigmatic saying of Matthew 11:12f. and Luke 16:16. W. G. Kümmel[69] has convincingly set forth the original form of this saying (later arranged in unnatural contexts): Luke 16:16a + Matthew 11:12 (or reversed). Also, the conception rules here that with the revelation of Christ (in which God's kingdom is present) the counter-kingdom also engages in distinct activity, with the goal of usurping the absolute lordship, the very position, of God himself!

---

64 It is therefore not correct to explain the retreat of the dragon from chapter 13 by saying that "its fate is decided" (Lohmeyer, *op. cit.*, p. 165), for it continues to work. There are christological, salvation-history grounds which bring about his retreat.

65 Volz, *op. cit.*, p. 88.

66 Cf. Heitmüller, *op. cit.*, pp. 85f. The ancient church certainly understood John 5:43 correctly (see the examples in W. Bauer, *Das Johannesevangelium, Hdb. L.*, Vol. 6, 3rd ed. [1933], p. 90); the passage is definitely not to be referred to a specific historical figure.

67 Cf. p. 65.

68 Cf. pp. 116ff.

69 W. G. Kümmel, *Promise and Fulfilment*, pp. 121–124.

The interpretation of the *biastai* given by M. Dibelius[70] as referring to demonic powers is very convincing.[71] If he is right, the Christian view of the function of the antichristian power amplified above is already at hand here.

If in 2 Corinthians 6:14-16 Beliar is to be understood as a type of the Antichrist, then Paul also sees the Antichrist as already in action in his own time. Nor does 2 Thessalonians 2:1-12 contradict this outlook on the intermediary time as the time of the Antichrist. Here the manifestation of the "man of lawlessness" is first expected in the future. But it points already to the present: *to gar mystērion ēdē energeitai tēs anomias*. There is thus distinguished a hidden and a visible working of the Antichrist. The intermediary time is until its final end the time of the hidden lordship of the Antichrist, "for (already) with Jesus' death and resurrection the End events have begun to move."[72] *Energeitai* excludes the conception of a purely passive existence. But this function in the world first becomes visible at the End. Paul certainly believes here that the revelation of the Antichrist would then occur in a distinct manner in a human figure.[73]

In the synoptic apocalypse there occurs the appearance of the Antichrist's power in connection with the destruction of Jerusalem and the establishment of the "desolating sacrilege" as a consequence of the rejection of Jesus (Mark 13:14 and parallels). The End is expected immediately or with the least delay after the appearance of the Antichrist (Mark 13:30).[74]

---

70 M. Dibelius, *Die urchristliche Ueberlieferung von Johannes dem Täufer*, pp. 26ff.

71 Cf. also Kümmel, *op. cit.*, p. 123, footnote 72: *"biastai* could . . . very well refer to spiritual powers hostile to God."

72 M. Dibelius, *Thessalonicher I. II./ Philipper*, p. 49, excursis on 2 Thessalonians 2:10.

73 Didache 16 speaks purely futuristically of the appearance of the Antichrist at the end of the old world's time. It thus stands even nearer to the Jewish Antichrist conception.

74 The interpretation of *hautē hē genea* is questionable, as is well known. Perhaps those contemporary with Jesus are meant (so E. Klostermann, *Das Markusevangelium*, *Hdb. L.*, Vol. 3, 3rd ed. [1936], *ad loc.;* he holds no particular position in any event), or the Jewish people, with whose continuance until the Parousia this would agree (cf. G. Dehn, *Jesus Christus Gottes Sohn*, and with him H. Bietenhard, *Das tausendjährige Reich* [1944]; J. Schniewind, *Das Markusevangelium*, *NTD*, Vol. 1, 4th ed. [1950], *ad loc.*, indicates that this solution might be possible). The then necessary reference to the withered fig tree (Mark 11:20–26; 13:28ff.) appears to me however to be still too uncertain. Lohmeyer (*Das Markusevangelium*, *Meyers Kommentarwerk*, 10th ed. [1937], *ad loc.*, p. 282) thinks—indeed, not only of a purely temporal designation for a generation—"rather, as usual, nearly always (of) a qualitative one: this evil and

The Johannine conception stands much the nearest to the Revelation, as in 1 John 2:18, 22; 4:3, and 2 John 7, where the Antichrist is seen in action during the entire intermediary time. This conception of the Antichrist is indistinguishable from that of the Revelation. First and Second John separate the Antichrists into singular and plural. In the plural form, the title of Antichrist designates human teachers of false doctrine. But it should not be overlooked that behind them stands the Antichrist (in the singular), who is understood as a supernatural, satanic person, who is (like his father, John 8:44) "the liar" (1 John 2:22). He sends out his evil spirit to his own people just as God sends the Holy Spirit. "In 1 John 4:1-3 the teachers of false doctrine are correctly designated as false prophets sent out into the world by the Antichrist."[75] Second John 7 is also to be understood unequivocally: the work of the supernatural Antichrist is the sending out of the "many deceivers." There is here no spiritualizing of the Antichrist conception as over against the rest of the New Testament. For from the beginning there is in the New Testament, adjacent to the political, a purely nonpolitical line of religious thought as well (cf. above, also Mark 13:5f. and parallels). The political view is more strongly influenced by the Jewish tradition, the nonpolitical developed as a fundamentally Christian view out of the experience of the Christ event. An alteration of the political understanding as over against Judaism has entered into the New Testament insofar as it is also understood from a purely religious viewpoint: any tie to nationalism is lacking, political religion is understood as one form of heathendom among others.

In any case, we see that the conception of the appearance of the Antichrist (simultaneously with that of Christ) in Revelation 12–13 does not present a picture completely distinguishable from that in the rest of the New Testament literature. In the Revelation the conception of the Antichrist formed by the historical Christ revela-

---

unfaithful generation will see that which the faithful recognize right now." To this the *eggys* of verse 29 would also correspond in its temporal meaning. Cf. also the carefully weighed investigation of W. Michaelis, *Der Herr verzieht nicht die Verheissung. Die Aussagen Jesu über die Nähe des jüngsten Tages* (1942), pp. 30ff.

75 Windisch, *op. cit., ad loc.*

tion is most distinctively stamped and hence stands at a great distance from Judaism.[76]

And so the whole intermediary time is, in the Revelation, the time of the battle of the Antichrist against Christ. The battle of the diabolical powers cannot be aimed thereby directly against Christ, for they have been banished out of heaven (ch. 12); rather, the battle is turned against his church: the dragon pursues the woman, 12:13, and, when she is found to be invulnerable, the rest of her offspring.[77]

Chapter 13 offers now a further carrying out of this persecution, which is accomplished by the Antichrist and his spirit. The battle pursues the religious goal of making the world into the church of the Antichrist (13:3f.; 12, 15). He who opposes this goal will be exterminated (13:10, 15; 11:7).

Just as Christ's work in the intermediary time is not restricted to the church alone but includes the whole of humanity, so also in the case of the Antichrist. This inclusive event of the End time is set forth in the series of visions of the first four seals, that of the apocalyptic riders. Above all, it is the first rider on the white horse with whom expositors have been most engrossed. But the widespread explanations referring to Christ, to his Word, or even to the Parthians, war, imperialism, etc., do not allow for the explanation of all the details and of the role of the first rider within the group as a whole.[78]

The overall conception of the four riders is influenced by the Old Testament patterns of plagues.[79] As the leader of a group who

---

76 Therefore there can be no talk of a Jewish source in chapters 12–13 (cf. Eb. Vischer, *Die Johannesoffenbarung eine jüdische Apokalypse?* [1895]).

77 A direct analogy to *potamophorēton poiēsē* (12:15) out of comparative religion has not been forthcoming; however, there is first to be noted the evil sense which the symbol of the flood denotes in the Old Testament (Pss. 18:4; 36:6; 124:4f.; Isa. 43:2); secondly, attention may be drawn to the fact that the serpent is often set forth as a water monster (Ezek. 29:3f.; 32:2f.; Ps. 74:13; Testament of Assher 7:3); but, thirdly, we note that in the myths of world destruction water is the element of annihilation (Gen. 6ff.; cf. Gunkel, *Genesis, ad loc.,* pp. 67ff., where more material from comparative religion is pointed out).

78 On the history of this exposition and on the many details, cf. my article in *Interpretation* 18, pp. 407–418.

79 Ezekiel 14:21; Jeremiah 15:2 (Lev. 26:21–26, where the same four elements appear together in a longer list of curses; they perhaps belonged originally to a sevenfold scheme); Zechariah 1:8–15. The striking correspondence of the seven seal visions with the pattern of seven signs found in the synoptic apocalypse likewise suggests dependence on a common tradition. Cf. my article, *ibid.,* pp. 413f.

initiate the final judgments (war, famine, tragic death),[80] the rider
on the white horse appears with the sign of his special function, the
bow.[81] The presentation is too general to allow reference to any
special people,[82] and as a symbol of Christ's salvation activity or of
the gospel, the bow and arrows are remarkably unfit. Christ's
weapon is the sword.[83] For this reason this image is not to be found
in the Old Testament and Jewish literature as a symbol of the saving
Word of God. The Old Testament speaks of God's bow only when
it appears as "the enemy."[84] There is, however, in the Old Testament a truly parallel figure that is decisive for the interpretation of
the rider on the white horse, namely, the mythical king in the Gog-
prophecy of Ezekiel 39, which Revelation 19:17-21 carries over to
the Antichrist (Ezek. 39:4, 6, 17–20). The last apocalyptic enemy
of God's people bears, according to Ezekiel 39:3, as the leader of
his hordes his characteristic weapon, the bow. Thus in the first rider
of Revelation 6 an image of the Antichrist is to be seen as well, he
who appears in various images (11:7; 13:17; 17:1ff.) and is already—as we have seen—in action during the entire End time. The
other two elements of the picture, the white color of the horse and
the victor's crown with the explanatory word, "he went out conquering and to conquer," belong to the imitation-motif of the
Antichrist theme.[85]

Hence this vision offers an opportunity to understand the other
plague series. In them all it is clearly not important to know in
what order the individual events take place, so that one could
reckon thereby the place of each in the world's time. Much more
are they designated by their organization in these schemes as genu-

---

80 See *ibid.*, p. 415.

81 All four figures are characterized by three marks of essence or function: the color
of the horse, a symbol disclosing purpose (bow, sword, balance, name), and an interpretation of activity (conquering, taking peace from the earth, raising the price of food,
killing).

82 The bow is not only the weapon of the Parthians but, in general, a feared weapon
of attack for the ancient nations. It is a part of the typical cavalry equipment of all
oriental armies and the particular weapon of the king and the generalissimo. See
K. Galling, *Biblisches Reallexikon* (1937), p. 116; Y. Yadin, *The Art of Warfare in
Biblical Lands,* 2 vols. (1963), *s.v.* bow.

83 Cf. W. Michaelis, *TWB* 6:696–698; T. Holtz, *op. cit.,* p. 179.

84 Genesis 9:13; Job 6:4; Psalm 38:2; Lamentations 2:4; 3:12; Habakkuk 3:9–14;
cf. Ephesians 6:16.

85 The more precise discussion of this is found in my article, *op. cit.,* pp. 416ff.

inely homogeneous. They define, with or after one another, the character of the intermediary time.

The Antichrist is further revealed in the vision of chapter 6 as the power who cooperates with and leads in the final catastrophes of history and the cosmos. War, hunger, death, entry into Hades, and human and cosmic catastrophes are his workings. The association of the eschatological plagues with the demonic powers is also emphasized in 9:2ff. and 16:13f.

This view of the Antichrist theme which is here unveiled is not unimportant for the definition of what Christian apocalyptic is and what goals it serves. Christian eschatology has not simply diverged from the Jewish form; it has a wholly new orientation and has thereby taken on an inner transformation. This transformation is present in the synoptic as well as in the Johannine apocalyptic. We recognize precisely from Revelation 6 that the apocalyptic elements in the Christian view were no longer, as in the Jewish view, tied to a secret knowledge which leads to the secrets of the cosmos and above all to an exact teaching about individual future events within history.

Therefore, the mention of traditional, apocalyptic occurrences in Christian eschatology does not allow the time and date of the End to be read off and calculated. Indeed, precisely Mark 13:32, which stands in connection with the synoptic apocalypse and which is so often understood on the basis of Jewish suppositions, forbids this apocalyptic reckoning.

Neither the fact nor the form of the individual events interests the Christian apocalyptist, but the wholly new sense which the events of the End time from the historical Christ event on, cited in traditional forms, contain. The new christocentric End-of-history-view of the intermediary time reveals its background and hidden associations. They are recognized as symptoms of the decisive battle of the spirits, of Christ and his counterpart, of the battle which has already been decided by the historical Christ event. The Christian apocalyptist is distinguished from the Jewish by this wholly new, christocentric understanding of the End time which exhibits the inner ground of all the occurrences of the End time. Because of this, the form of these events has lost its decisive worth and is no longer useful for purposes of calculation. Hence, to separate Jesus himself from the apocalyptic thought in Mark 13 and parallels or the Revelation of John on grounds of content criticism[86] is not necessary although the form of the outcome which the eschatological thinking has found here stems out of the tradition and even if there is otherwise to be found in the "tradition of Jesus' eschatological preaching no (direct) parallel."[87]

In the passages dealt with up to now we have come to know the Antichrist as a supernatural spiritual power. The decisive battle against Christ finds consummation now however in the view of the Revelation, not only in the supernatural regions, but on earth. This concrete, earthly battle is consummated in such a manner that the Antichrist makes use of mankind for the achievement of his goal and makes mankind his possession.

In the discussion of the Antichrist in 13:1-10, we had already pointed to chapter 17, for the figures of the beast are very similar in both sections. And yet they do not appear to be simply identical. Chapter 17 shows the beast inseparably bound up with the harlot Babylon; the seven heads and ten horns are spoken of, although the diadems are lacking. The whole beast (not just the heads as in chapter 13) is full of blasphemous names. But the decisive point is that in chapter 17 the fatal wound is lacking, the factor which stamps the figure of the Antichrist in chapter 13. The "is not" of the beast cannot be identified with his being killed, for it involves only a temporary retreat into the underworld, from which he returns again.

The correspondences of the two beast images appear, however, to show that chapter 17 intends to speak to the Antichrist power as well.[88]

A direct association of the two figures is established by the enigmatic number in 13:18: "its number is six hundred and sixty-

---

86 Cf. W. G. Kümmel, *op. cit.*, pp. 95–104.
87 *Ibid.*, p. 101.
88 That John in chapters 13 and 17 is depending on different traditions may be true, although it does not explain what he himself wished to express with the peculiar correspondences and simultaneous differences in the images. That he himself had something in mind is to be assumed, if we do not—as Joh. Munck once said so well—"wish to brand [him] as an intellectual imbecile" (*Petrus und Paulus in der Offenbarung Johannis. Ein Beitrag zur Auslegung der Apokalypse, Teolokiske Skrifter* 1 [1950], p. 31).

six."[89] Interpretations of the number have been given in great profusion.[90] But most of them are altogether too frivolous. It is difficult to decide whether it is a purely arithmetic number or a riddle of the gematria sort and whether Hebrew or Greek letters are to be used. Yet there are two possibilities which seem to me to have the greatest probability of being true. One is the suggestion of G. A. van den Berg van Eysinga concerning triangular number speculations: "in every triangular number there lies the same meaning as in the last member of the series." Now the sum of all the numbers $1-36 = 666$ and $1-8 = 36$, so that the interpretation of the number 666 is the same as that of 8.[91] Thus the number 666 points forward to an "eighth," which actually appears in Revelation 17:11.[92]

A second interpretation, which perhaps from the very beginning has been combined with the one just now sketched out, is the familiar gematria referring to Nero.[93] The solution of the enigmatic number would then mean: take note of it when again the Antichrist is spoken of in a later part of the book. He will appear there as the eighth, as the human embodiment or the human instrument of the "beast" of chapter 13! And if the second interpretation is right, it can only be a reference to the Nero myth: the eighth will be the reappearing Nero!

I believe that the majority of interpreters rightly see in chapter 17 (in contrast to chapter 13!) a political interpretation of the Antichrist. Lohmeyer, to the contrary, has pointed to the anchoring of nearly all the elements of the text in traditional outlooks, so that the derivation of many details of the image out of the contemporary situation is largely superfluous. But Lohmeyer is not successful in giving a uniform and clear derivation of the whole image out of

---

89 This is certainly the original number as over against 616. "A human number" is to be explained by analogy to 21:17 as a "man's measure."

90 Cf. my article "666" in the *Biblisch-Historischen Wörterbuch*.

91 "Dic in der Apk. bekämpfte Gnosis," *ZNW* 13 (1912), pp. 293–305. But he connects with this the gnostic Sophia speculations, which are remote from the Revelation.

92 Cf. Th. Zahn, *op. cit.*, p. 502.

93 The defective writing *nrwn qsr* is now attested in an Aramaic document from the second year of the emperor Nero, *CDJD* II, No. 18, Plate XXIX. "The last two consonants of *qsr* are damaged, but enough is preserved to show that no vowel-letter was written between the *q* and *s*" (D. R. Hillers, "Revelation 13:18 and the Scrolls from Murabba'at," *Bulletin of the American Schools of Oriental Research* 170 [1963], p. 65).

the tradition, and, above all, the doors to a contemporary explanation of single motifs of the image yet remain open. Lohmeyer, noting the designation of the "ten kings" (cf. Dan. 7:20, 24), even points to the fact that they could be the product of "a rationalizing of originally demonic figures." In this connection he draws attention to 1 Corinthians 2:8. And this really appears to be a parallel which can contribute a decisive part in the clarification of chapters 17 and 18. Here, as there, the human-supernatural character of the demonic operation in human history is pointed out. This is the basis for the peculiar, inextricable intertwining of two distinct lines of thought in chapters 17 and 18: the supernatural-demonic, which stamps the whole scene in traditional colors, and the human, which shows itself especially in the explanations found within the text.[94]

We have to discuss first of all the special structure of chapter 17. Only here we find a great deal of particularizing and forced explanations of the vision figures bound up with unevenness of presentation.

We can distinguish the following parts:

1. 17:1-2. An angel proclaims the sight of the judgment on the "great harlot," who is characterized as Babylon with words from the Old Testament.[95]

2. Then John is shown in a vision image the nature of Babylon (17:3-6). The Seer is carried away to a desert (cf. the introduction to the speech on Babylon in Isa. 21:1!). He sees the woman, laden with adornments, sitting on the beast. The woman bears a name which indicates her mystery: "mother of harlots and of earth's abominations." She is the midpoint of a world at enmity with God. Thus, the actual city is not meant, but Babylon as a type.[96] And by the association with the "beast" Babylon is drawn into the Antichrist theme in a special way. Babylon is the city and the kingdom of the Antichrist, in which God's people are persecuted (17:6).[97] And here again the counter-image motif is in play, for

---

[94] O. Cullmann, *The State in the New Testament* (1956), pp. 89–92.
[95] Harlotry, as often in the Old Testament, is the same as idolatry. "Upon many waters" is from Jeremiah 51:13; the drunkenness of the nations, from Jeremiah 51:7.
[96] Cf. K. G. Kuhn, *TWB* 1:512ff.
[97] See *ibid.*, 1:514.

the woman is clearly the counter-image of the woman clothed with the sun (12:1; cf. 3:17f.; 19:7-9). Hence, Babylon, as the church of the Antichrist, cannot be exclusively a demonic reality; rather, as the church of Christ, it is a human society.

3. To this vision of Babylon and its beast there is joined on an explanation of both great personages by an angel. This third part now shows all manner of unevennesses and lack of clarity. After verse 9a, a separate word of admonition, there is an explanation primarily of the beast, followed by a further, detailed, allegorical interpretation, which in its form and fullness of detail departs completely from all the interpretations of the images explained in the Revelation. The double interpretation of the seven heads as hills and kings is quite singular. If this is the case, this interpretation dissolves the unity of the image of the beast and its heads; if the heads are understood as a succession of kings maintained by the beast, it would certainly not be present at the time of the sixth and seventh kings (17:10), but would have existed earlier and would appear again as the eighth. This interpretation comes to pieces, however, in the context of the vision image, as an eighth king appears here beyond the seven heads.

Also out of place is the interpretation of "the waters that you saw," on which the prostitute is seated (17:15). For John has certainly not seen them; they belong to the words in which the angel announced the vision, describing the reality to be seen with Old Testament terms (as often in the Revelation). But in the vision Babylon appears in the desert, sitting on the beast! Woman and beast constitute in the vision a perfect unity, so that the now appended saying about the destruction of the prostitute by the ten kings and the beast seems more than peculiar.

And, finally, when we compare this overly long explanation of the beast with the brief discussion of the woman, we must hold grave doubts about the place of the explanation of the beast in the original text.

When we seek after the intrusive material in the present textual arrangement, the original wording can be recovered without difficulty. Corresponding to the other explanations of vision images,

which are all kept very clear, simple, and brief,[98] there would follow also here, according to the proclamation in 17:7, a brief explanation of the beast: the beast was, but is not there now,[99] and
yet will return from the underworld. All the world except God's
people will then marvel. But the Seer and the church, who know
the mystery of the beast, are aware that the fate of the beast has
already been sealed and that he cannot escape ruin. The admoni-
tory words of 17:9a instruct the reader to pay due attention to
this when the beast, already in action once, appears again.

What then follows in 17:9b-17 proves to be a later inserted,
hybrid extension of the interpretation. In verse 18 we have the
original continuation of verse 9a.[100] The woman is explained as
the empress of the world, the one who "has dominion over the
kings of the earth."[101] This shows that we doubtless have to do
with a political interpretation of the figure of the Antichrist and
his community. Babylon is, of course, the Roman empire according to Jewish apocalyptic tradition.[102] Thus for John, Babylon per-
sonifies the Antichrist and will again personify him who "was, and
is not, and is to ascend from the bottomless pit." The power of
Antichrist on earth is at home in the political sphere in a special
way, insofar as the worldly kingdom becomes a religious power
which makes a total demand on men and forces them to conform
to its godless life: who will not drink from her cup (17:4; 18:3),
commit fornication with her (a clear reference to idolatry out of
the Old Testament, 17:5; 18:3, 9), and take part in her self-
glorification (17:4; 18:7) and her unrighteous wealth (17:4; 18:3,
11-17), would withdraw from her (18:4!), will be slain (17:6;
18:24).

Taken by itself, the "mystery of . . . the beast" who "was, and
is not," will return and "go to perdition," is now thoroughly ex-

---

98 Revelation 1:20 (here as in 17:7: the image without explanation is a mystery!);
7:14.

99 *Ouk estin* does not mean "he does not exist," but "he is not there," because, as
verse 8 shows, he had temporarily retreated to the bottomless pit (17:10).

100 Cf. the parallelism: "the beast that you saw . . ."
                         "the woman that you saw . . ."

101 The "kings of the earth" are the embodiment of all the political power of the
world (16:14; 19:19). Notice that no reference is made to the ten kings of the secondary interpretation!

102 Syriac Baruch 67:7; Sibylline Oracles 5:143; cf. 1 Peter 5:13.

plainable from the historical experience of the Seer and the Jewish-Christian expectation of a full revelation of the Antichrist at the End of time. The beast has already revealed itself in the Roman empire in the past. It is to be assumed that John has in mind Nero's persecution. At the time of the book's writing he does not see the beast in action, but expects it in the future. Presuming that the Nero myth in the form of Nero's return from the underworld was known in Asia Minor already, John is alluding to it. It is striking that in the whole context no word is spoken of the emperor cult, which shows that it did not yet play any role for Christians in Asia Minor at the time of the book's writing.

Now we may pay attention to the secondary interpretation found in 17:9b-17, which will yield some interesting associations. This later interpretation has the obvious aim of expounding the originally clear prophetic message directed toward the future to the historical situation of its own time, and of showing that it was being fulfilled in its own days. From this may be explained the peculiar tension between the vision image (17:3-6), the original interpretation (17:7-9a, 18), and the temporal application now constructed from it. This is an attempt to connect the mystery of the beast, who is active in the past and future but not in the present, with the allegorizing of the heads as a sequence of seven or, possibly, eight kings. Moreover, historical reality would demand the insertion of an eighth. The original characterizing of the beast in 17:8a also serves this secondary interpretation as an indication of the fact that the Roman state at no time, thus also under the sixth and seventh caesars, is simply to be identified with the beast from the abyss, but is to be found only in its individual representatives.[103]

We positively find here also the myth of *Nero redivivus* being employed, for the eighth should already have been one of the seven (more precisely, according to 17:10-11, one of the first five). And to this there also belongs the added interpretation of the ten horns, corresponding to the satraps of the Nero myth who are to help in Rome's destruction of the returning Roman emperor

---

103 The double reference to seven kings and seven hills is a further cue, pointing to Rome, the city of seven hills.

(17:16f.). The enigmatic number of 13:18b is also now applied to the secondary interpretation. Its position at the end of the vision of the second beast of chapter 13 is quite striking (although it refers to the first beast). With the word of admonition, *hōde hē sophia estin,* the portrayal of the second beast is concluded, formally entirely parallel to the conclusion of the vision of the first beast, *hōde estin hē hypomonē kai hē pistis tōn hagiōn* (13:10). Right at the end of the whole scene, after the vision of the second beast, the enigmatic number has been later attached, which—as we have seen—draws attention to the secondary interpretation of chapter 17 and even tempts us to interpret the beast of chapter 13 politically. The name with a number is also attached to the beast in 15:2.

We possess in these verses of the secondary interpretation the only really useful historical statement that enables us perhaps to specify the date of the book's authorship. The main question is, naturally, with which emperor must the numbering begin. Now, in the old church tradition according to Irenaeus (*adv. haer.* 5:30:3), the Revelation is very precisely dated in the time of Domitian. It is evident that for the church, Domitian, the persecutor of the Christians, was feared as the eighth, the full revelation of the Antichrist. If we now count backwards from Domitian, we find an astonishingly accurate synchronization of the allusions given by the secondary interpretation with historical reality. To the seventh emperor only a short time of rule is assigned (17:10!): Titus ruled only two years. Then the sixth is Vespasian. That Vespasian and Titus are not identified for the Christian interpreters of history with the beast from the abyss is completely justifiable.[104] To number the emperor of the interregnum in this list of official representatives of the world kingdom is certainly not right. Thus Nero is to be numbered as the fifth, and with Claudius, Caligula, and Tiberius, we come to Augustus as the first of the series.

For the starting point of the reckoning there is however also— as has been made clear in the preceding investigation—an objec-

---

104 "That Vespasian had assigned any special emphasis to the emperor cult (Giet, *op. cit.,* p. 122) speaks against all that we know" (W. G. Kümmel, *Einleitung in das Neue Testament,* p. 342).

tively grounded indication. John considers the Antichrist to be at work during the whole intermediary time since the historical Christ event. Hence the first ruler is also for the secondary interpretation to be sought in the time of the beginning of the revelation of Christ. Thus we come to the enumeration which begins with Augustus.

The ancient church's dating, at least that of the secondary interpretation, is thereby confirmed and that apparently means a second edition of the book in the time of Domitian. Who had inserted 13:18b; 15:2 ("and the number of its name"); 17:9b-17, we do not know. Certainly not John himself, for it does not correspond to his style.[105]

More important however is the question of why in the secondary interpretation the writing of the book is dated back in the time of the sixth emperor (17:10), thus in the time of Vespasian. This problem is quite understandable if we assume that the anonymous writer, who saw his own time prophesied as the "last" in the Revelation and wished to make the others known by his additions, knew the original time of writing quite precisely and therefore dated his *vaticinium ex eventu* back to this time![106]

We win by this a strong foothold for the dating of the book. According to 17:10 ("the other has not yet come") the appearance of the seventh king is imminently expected, so that we have to assume as the time of authorship the end of Vespasian's rule.[107]

To this explanation of the intermediary time as the time of the Antichrist there is tied a motif of historical-theological significance

---

105 The redactor has formed the victory of Christ in 17:14 after 19:11ff.: the two titles of Christ stem from 19:16; the angelic hosts of 19:14 are here made into a reference to the church; 17:14 speaks of a future victory of the Lamb, which never otherwise occurs in the Revelation, for Christ as the Lamb is victorious once for all (5:5, 9; 12:11; 3:21), the returning one appears as the judge to whom all are already subjugated! To that cf. my article, *ThZ* 2 (1965), pp. 81ff.

106 Feuillet's surmise (*NTS* 4 [1958], p. 200) that John himself had backdated his book to before the destruction of Jerusalem in order to make clear the theological significance of that event does not have very evident grounds. He could have accomplished this without the device of backdating. And one ought not forget that he was not writing for the Palestinian church!

107 It appears to me that in the whole book there is no single circumstance which speaks against the early date of its writing (cf. also Hadorn, *op. cit.,* pp. 221f.). And thus it may be explained that while there is no trace of the cult of caesar or state persecution in the provincial churches (to whom the seven letters were directed), yet Rome —under the impress of the Neronic persecution, whose memory had not yet faded out— has been judged to be the power of the Antichrist and it can be described in 17:6 as already drunk with the blood of the martyrs of Jesus.

which ties the Revelation to the interpretation of history of the rest of the New Testament as well as to Judaism. Judaism's view of history carries a "pessimistic" strain in its attitude toward the development of humanity within history.[108] The powers arrayed against God expand in an intensive and extensive progression, leading to the final great battle in which God himself engages.[109] The Revelation also exhibits this line of thought. The Antichrist, already raging on the earth since Christ's appearance, reveals himself at the end of the intermediary time with special clarity and totality. The seventeenth chapter has already showed us that. This perception also clearly lies at the basis of 11:7, where certainly nothing of the work of the Antichrist during the whole intermediary time is reflected;[110] rather, it emphasizes the intensifying of his function and its being pointed against the church during the final battle. The victory of the Antichrist is emphasized with great force in 11:7. God's cause is apparently denied at the End.[111] The last great intensification of the battle with the Antichrist is also expected in 3:10. It brings for the church the great future temptation which comes "on the whole world." Then the "tribulation," which is present during the whole intermediary time (cf. 1:9; 2:9; 7:14), becomes all-inclusive.[112]

The final expansion and intensifying of the battle against God immediately before the "day of God" is set forth in the scene

---

108 According to whether a national or universal attitude is dominant, the ever increasing distress toward the End is, in Jewish literature, either limited to Israel or related to the Gentiles.

109 This historical view comes very clearly to light in the scheme of the kingdoms of Daniel 2. Cf. also Bousset, *Religion des Judentums*, pp. 230–256, and *Antichrist*, p. 145; Volz, *op. cit.*, Section 31.

110 However, this does not justify assuming that a new source has been worked in. Even less proper is the deletion of these verses (Spitta, *op. cit.*, pp. 226–228). That the beast was introduced before chapter 13 has its basis, not in a special "authentic tradition" (Bousset, *Die Offenbarung Johannes*, pp. 324ff.), but is intelligible from the construction of the whole book: chapter 11 constitutes an interlude which handles the whole intermediary time from a special aspect. That the Seer so defines the "beast" and can introduce him without further clarification is comprehensible since he ties it to a known Antichrist tradition. In particular, there stands behind this image the tradition which expects the appearance of the Antichrist in the End time in Jerusalem: Assumption of Moses 8—9; Mark 13:14ff.; Matthew 24:15; 2 Thessalonians 2:4; cf. Irenaeus, *adv. haer.* 5:30:4; Apocalypse of Elijah (Steindorff, *op. cit.*, p. 161). Cf. also Bousset, *Antichrist*, pp. 104f. *To anabainon ek tēs abyssou* is a description of the beast's nature and does not signify that he will first appear at the end of the 1260 days.

111 This victory is announced in 6:2 and alluded to in 13:15 also.

112 The intensity of the last "tribulation" is also emphasized in the synoptic testimony: Mark 13:19 and parallels.

showing the gathering of all the hosts of the satanic powers (sixth bowl, 16:12-16).

God's enemies appear chiefly as "the kings from the east" who stand ready beyond the Euphrates. The "great river Euphrates," the primitive eastern boundary of Israel, the ancient people of God (Gen. 15:18; Deut. 1:7; Joshua 1:4), has become in the Revelation the invasion stream of God's enemies. The conceptions which are bound up with the Euphrates have lost all their geographical associations, so that the river has also become the place of origin for the fantastic demonic hordes of 9:14-19.[113] At the End, the river is dried up to open the way to the enemy.

The enemy from the east is moreover only the vanguard. The satanic "trinity" calls together the "kings of the whole world," using demonic spirits "like frogs"[114] who have been sent out. All this is the preparation for the conclusive battle, which the Parousia scene of 19:19 describes.

The place of the great assembly of all the allies of the Antichrist's powers is again not geographically fixed, but is described by a term of mystery: Armageddon. The name is not explainable with complete certainty.[115] To me, the most convincing is the derivation from *har mo'ed,* "mount of assembly"[116] (from Isa. 14:13).

---

113 It is therefore most improbable that John, in 16:12, is thinking of the Parthians as in Ethiopian Enoch 55:5-6.

114 Cf. the plague of frogs in Exodus 8:1f.; Psalms 78:45; 105:30. In Parsiism frogs are the representatives of Ahriman.

115 To read "mount of Megiddo" is impossible, for the pre-New Testament literature knows only a plain of Meggido (2 Chron. 35:22; Zech. 12:11); Lohmeyer's reference to Carmel is equally impossible (on this, J. Jeremias, "Har Magedon," *ZNW* 31 [1932], pp. 73ff.); unlikely also is the combination of two Old Testament thoughts: Megiddo as the place of decisive engagement and the final battle on the "mountain of Israel" (Allo, *op. cit., ad loc.*). The "mountain of Migron" (Isa. 10:28ff., where Megiddo lies instead of Migron in LXX), suggested by van der Woude (*op. cit.*, pp. 180f.), is only a place of passage for the enemy and without any special eschatological meaning.

116 Cf. Jeremias, *op. cit.*, pp. 73-77, and *TWB* 1:467f. The single linguistic difficulty, the representation of Hebrew *'ayin* with Greek *gamma,* is not insurmountable; cf. Br. Violet, "Har Magedon," *ZNW* 31 (1932), pp. 205f. Also, there appears to me to be a real dependence traceable to Isaiah 14:13. Both passages speak in the language of myth, with a peculiar interweaving of event having a demonic background and historical foreground, as we have often previously encountered in the Revelation. (Cf. K. L. Schmidt, *ThZ,* Part 3 [1951], especially pp. 166ff.). Isaiah 14:13 stands in a song of triumph over the casting down to the realm of death of the great king of Babylon, who had yearned to set his throne above the stars on the "mount of assembly." In view of the fact that for the Revelation Babylon is a type of the Antichrist's kingdom, and moreover that in Isaiah 14:12 the demonic great king is named the "Day Star" (in the Revelation used as a name of Christ,

close association of the concepts of royal lordship and priesthood[120] no doubt points to the understanding of the church as object and subject of lordship.[121] The church receives a share in Jesus' rule (cf. Dan. 7:18; 1 Cor. 4:8; 1 Peter 2:5, 9).

The nature of the church is presented pictorially in the call vision of 1:12-20. John sees the seven churches as seven lampstands surrounding the divine Son of Man. Christ, the eschatological world ruler and judge with the sword, is already present in his church. The seven stars in his right hand, also a symbol of his rule,[122] are the angels of the churches, the organs by which Christ reigns over his church.[123]

That the churches are represented as lampstands connects well with the Old Testament conception of the temple lampstands. This is shown in 11:4, where the symbol for the two witnesses appears and reference is made to Zechariah 4:2, 11. The one lampstand of Zechariah 4:2 is, however, doubled. The basis for this we are yet to become acquainted with. Thus the two lampstands, together with the olive trees, i.e., the anointed of Zechariah, become two figures of the two witnesses.[124] The number seven in 1:12 indicates the circle of lampstands as the fullness of the whole messianic congregation.

Christ rules, however, not only in, but also through, his church,

---

120 After Exodus 19:6; cf. 1 Peter 2:9; Mekilta of Exodus 19:6 (71a).

121 Cf. L. Goppelt, "Heilsoffenbarung und Geschichte nach der Offenbarung des Johannes," *ThLZ* (1952), pp. 517f.

122 See E. Lohmeyer, *op. cit.*, p. 16.

123 The angels of the churches are certainly not men; the linguistic usage and the high position this would imply for men would be unique in the Revelation, and 1:20 excludes that "angel" is a symbolic word for star. They are like the angels of 1:1 and 14:6, transmitters of messages which must be written down for every church.

124 Tree and man are readily associated in oriental thought: cf. Jeremiah 11:19; Psalm 1:3; Job 29:19; Daniel 4; of the olive tree, Psalm 52:8; Jeremiah 11:16; Hosea 14:6. Exodus 25 is easily recognizable as the original association of the lampstand with the tree of life (tubes of the lamps as almond flowers). On the Jewish interpretations of the temple lampstands, cf. Philo, *Quaest. in Exodus* 2:71ff.; Josephus, *Ant.* 3:6, 7. On messianic interpretations (Midrash of Exodus Rabba 40:5; Numbers Rabba 15:4, 10, and the menora symbols on the graves of the Monteverde catacombs), see E. L. Ehrlich, *Kultsymbolik im Alten Testament und im nachbiblischen Judentum* (1959), pp. 94–96; cf. W. Eltester, "Der siebenarmige Leuchter und der Titusbogen," *ZNW* Beiheft 26, *Festschrift für J. Jeremias* (1960), pp. 62–76. The Zechariah passage has quite a special meaning in the two-messiah conception of the Qumran community (cf. K. G. Kuhn, "Die beiden Messias Aarons und Israels," *NTS* 1 [1960], pp. 168–170; J. Gnilka, *op. cit.*, pp. 395–426). R. B. Laurin, "The Problem of the 2 Messiahs in the Qumran Scrolls," *Revue de Qumran* 5 (1963), pp. 39–52, denies the two-messiah teaching for Qumran, but cannot solve the problems which then arise; cf. especially van der Woude, *op. cit.*

so far as it "holds the testimony of Jesus," i.e., proclaims him as the lord. Thus the church is the place within which redemption occurs and from which redemption goes out into the world. But because redemption is the final basis for the Lamb's world lordship (5:5f.) and because conversion is the intention of all the judgments of world history (9:20f.; 16:9, 11), the church is the essential center of Christ's lordship and of the history of the End time, and the position of the world in relation to it is the criterion of its position with God (12–14). Life and death are decided at the testimony of the church (11:5-6).

The Revelation, however, does not busy itself with making a display of the working of the word of salvation in the world, but rather with the strengthening of the church, which is surrounded by the world as by an enemy's impenetrable wall—and its testimony in the Antichrist's counterattack must be paid for with its life. It will know that its death is intimately associated with the testimony of the slain lord, because disdain of God's people indicates disdain of God (13:6f.).[125] But it shall also know that its victory reveals itself precisely in its defeat (12:11), for it stands in the Lamb's book of life (13:8). Thus it stakes its existence in the imitation of the Lamb (13:10).[126]

The existence and nature of this church of the End time is now set forth in four further major visions. We shall discuss primarily two scenes of the sealed (7:1-8 and 14:1-5).

At first, John sees in the interlude of chapter 7 the angels of the four winds of the earth who will bring the comprehensive End time catastrophes (cf. Dan. 7:2; Ethiopian Enoch 34:3; 76:4). But before this last time of devastation begins, God's people are sealed with the name of God and the Lamb, whose property they are decreed to be and under whose care they are placed (9:4; 14:1).[127]

---

125 Even the Jewish apocalypses base the persecution of God's people in this way, while rabbinic Judaism understands the suffering of the righteous as having atoning value. Cf. Ed. Schweizer, *Lordship and Discipleship* (1960), pp. 22ff.; W. D. Davies, *Paul and Rabbinic Judaism* (1948), pp. 259ff.; D. Rössler, *op. cit.*, pp. 91–95.

126 To be read with the best manuscripts according to Jeremiah 15:2; cf. J. Schmid, *Studien zur Geschichte des griechischen Apokalypse-Textes*, Part 2 (1955), pp. 138f.

127 Cf. pp. 43ff. Psalm of Solomon 15:6 also knows of a sign of eschatological salvation. Here there is in mind, in addition to preservation from hunger, sword, and death, preservation from the last judgment as well; cf. verses 12f. (yet cf. Volz, *op. cit.*, p. 304). 2 Esdras 6:5 also speaks of a sealing (at the beginning of the world). The basic Old Testament passages referring to this are: Ezekiel 9:4, 6; Isaiah 44:5.

Those sealed are in any event not externally free from the eschatological plague events; indeed, they live in "tribulation." But they are protected from the apostasy of the demons and the Antichrist. An apostasy is expected for the End time in a special way as the eschatological omen.[128] It takes place after the Christ event, provoked by the great persecution. In the final time the apostasy will be increased in the great "trial" (3:10). However, the sealing promises preservation and protection in the midst of all oppression (1:9), all plagues, so that those sealed are given "patience and endurance" for all events of the End time.[129] Hence those sealed can be termed the *nikōntes* (cf. 2:7; 15:2, and other passages). In the image of the sealing, the same promise is visible which is expressed in I Clement 59:2.

Who belongs to the 144,000 people of God? The enumerating of the tribes of Israel could refer to the old twelve-tribe people or to Jewish-Christianity. But this is not possible. According to 9:4, all need the seal who would not fall into the power of the demons, and the designation of the 144,000 as "servants of our God" is generally used for the church of Jesus.[130]

The Christian church has, according to the New Testament, understood itself as the new Israel (Rom. 2:29; Gal. 3:29; 6:16; Phil. 3:3; 1 Peter 1:1; James 1:1; Herm. Sim. 9:17:1). Thus it is not at all strange when John not only transfers the Old Testament "my people" to the church (18:4; 21:3), but the image of the twelve-tribe people as well. The reference to the structure of the people of Israel is a meaningful allusion to the special association of old and new Israel, into which we have yet to inquire.

The limitation of the church by the number 144,000 discloses its character as marked out, bought (14:4), called, and chosen.[131] The existence of the church depends on the grace of election (1:5;

---

128 Cf. Enoch 90:7ff.; 93:9; Apocalypse of Baruch 28:3; 2 Esdras 13:16ff.; Babylonian Talmud Shabbath 138b; Matthew 24:10; 2 Thessalonians 2:3; 1 Timothy 4:1; 1 John 2:18ff.

129 Cf. E. Lohmeyer, *Das Vater-Unser*, p. 145. They are those "who by God's power are guarded" (1 Peter 1:5).

130 1:1; 2:20; 6:11; 19:2, 5; 22:3f., 6. Individual passages show that they retain the Old Testament prophetic meaning (1:1; 10:7; 11:18): the Christian church is the church of the Spirit.

131 17:14. Cf. also the image of the book of life, 13:8; 17:8; 20:15; 21:27; cf. Romans 11:25f. See W. C. van Unnik, "Le nombre des élus dans la première épitre de Clément," *RHPR* 42 (1962), pp. 237–246.

5:9f.). It lives only by the word which has been given it (2–3) as the church of him who is the word of God himself (19:13). But that indicates that it is placed in the decisive position wherein it must preserve the word and thereby testify to its election (1:3, 9; 12:17; 14:12).

This reality of life of the elect is made visible in the other image of the 144,000 (14:1-5). They have maintained their election in their encounter with the powers of this world (14:12f.). Their location on earth is called by John the mountain of Zion, for where the Lamb stands with his church is where the messianic kingdom is present.[132] The church therefore is able already to join in the new, eschatological song that accompanies it from heaven.

The whole scene is certainly not rightly understood if it is taken as the "Seer's ideal of the Lamb's consummated church."[133] The Seer shows not only "what must be," he gives not only "a hortatory pattern for the faithful on earth," but he shows the real character of the church, exactly as he sees it in the congregations of Asia Minor, and in whose midst—even as here—Christ stands (1:13). In spite of any doubtfulness, so long as they cling to the name of Christ in faith and are repentant, they positively are ransomed from the earth, drawn up out of mankind as the multitude of the redeemed, belonging no more to Satan and Antichrist, but to God and the Lamb.[134]

The same thing holds as well of the ethical assertions which are made here about the redeemed (14:4f.). On the ground of their association with the Lamb the redeemed acquire the enumerated qualities. For they are bought by the blood of the Lamb who has wrought forgiveness (1:5; 7:14; 22:14). The elect are therefore "virginal." *Parthenoi* cannot indicate asceticism,[135] for precisely

---

132 Cf. Joel 2:32; 2 Esdras 13:35: "But he [the Messiah] will stand on the top of Mount Zion"; 2:42ff.; Hebrews 12:22.

133 Lohmeyer, *Die Offenbarung des Johannes*, p. 120.

134 In 14:14, *tō arniō* is certainly original, since it is only maintained here that they are redeemed and belong to God and to the Lamb, while in 5:9 the ground of their redemption ("by thy blood . . . for God") is emphasized. Cf. 1 Corinthians 6:20; 7:23; 2 Peter 2:1; Galatians 3:13; 4:5, and Mandaean Liturgy 75, "thou hast predestined us and lifted us out of the world of the enemy." (Cf. A. Deissmann, *op. cit.*, pp. 270–281.)

135 See S. Giet, *op. cit.*, pp. 142f., who thinks of a reworking of an Essene text which spoke of the celibacy of the saved community.

in the Revelation is marriage invested with the highest value in the image of the marriage of the Lamb (19:7f.; 21:2; 22:17). And with this Old Testament image of the church (Hos. 2:14-21; Jer. 2:2-6), which is referred to Christ and those who are his (initially found in the New Testament in 2 Cor. 11:2), the whole expression is hung together. But the image has experienced a certain transformation, insofar as the conception of the tribes of Israel lies at its root, for their representatives in the Old Testament are all *men.* Thus the masculine form *hoi parthenoi* has to be used here and, correspondingly, the formula "these who have not defiled themselves with *women."* Thus the whole expression designates the church of the Lamb as the pure people of God, free from idolatry. The positive antithesis is: they follow only the Lamb "wherever he goes."[136] As such followers, they are blameless.

As the warnings of the Revelation show, especially the call to repentance in the letters to the churches, this indicative image of the church's "form of kerygmatic essence"[137] is at the same time bound up with the imperative: become what you are. The whole book makes it quite clear that defection from God's law is not the basic sin, but unrepentance, which excludes forgiveness and renewing grace (2:5, 16, 21; 3:3, 18f.).

The messianic congregation, whose eschatological nature is emphasized, is indeed the church which still lives in the old aeon, yet lives in the temptation of its own sins (cf. the messages to the churches), and which must be admonished. It is a church which stands in the persecution of Satan and Antichrist, which can even be defeated by them outwardly (11:7; 13:7), which not only rules as a royal kingdom and can do its priestly service (1:6, 9), which shares in eternal life not only right now, but which also must still live in "tribulation"[138] that intensifies the nearer the End comes. Hence it must still protect its redeemed position and certify it in many trials, even as far as death. The church before the Parousia

---

136 Cf. Ed. Schweizer, *op. cit.,* pp. 20ff.
137 L. Goppelt, *op. cit.,* p. 518.
138 The "tribulation" or the "great tribulation" (1:9; 7:14) characterizes the whole End time. It is the "time which creates trouble" (Syriac Baruch 48:31) as Judaism had expected. So also speak Daniel 12:10; Matthew 24:9f.; Mark 13:19; Shepherd of Hermas, Vision IV, 3:6.

is still the *hidden* messianic kingdom, which is first comprehensible in faith. The consummation, union with the Lord, awaits the Parousia.

The two other vision images of the church show that nothing can be said of the position and meaning of the church in the history of the End time without insight into its complex nature, which involves fulfillment and promise at the same time.

We had previously observed in 7:1-8 that the church is designated as the true Israel, heir of the promises. For the Revelation, "Jew" is no invective, but a name of honor which the synagogue could no longer properly bear (2:9; 3:9).[139]

It is doubtless clear here that *Ioudaios* for the Christian apocalyptist indicates the highest predicate of honor, a term which is not appropriate to a Judaism which remains at enmity with the Christian church. The polemic designation *hē synagōgē tou satana* opens up the legitimate claim which, in the apocalyptist's opinion, true Judaism may advance, that is, to be *hē synagōgē tou theou,* the community of God. The prerogatives of salvation history, with which the idea of "Jew" is bound up, are taken with complete seriousness by the writer and their validity acknowledged for the present time. For, that the Judaism of the two cities, Smyrna and Philadelphia, is no longer legitimately addressed by the honored name *Ioudaioi,* does not lead to the conclusion that this special claim no longer exists in the time of the Christian church, but rather that the Jews in question do not meet the associated demand. The Seer thus distinguishes—as does Paul—the true Jew to whom the promise of salvation is directed from him who is one only in an external sense. "For he is not a real Jew who is one outwardly . . . He is a Jew who is one inwardly" (Rom. 2:28f.).

---

139 The same salvation meaning for the name "Jew" holds in John 4:22, which (in spite of W. Bauer, *op. cit., ad loc.,* and R. Bultmann, *op. cit., ad loc.*) is no mere gloss. The *humeis* are "Samaritans who have acted as representatives of the Gentile power" (Holtzmann, *Das Johannesevangelium, Handkommentar zum NT,* ed. W. Bauer [1890], *ad loc.*); with *hēmeis* Jesus reckons himself as part of Israel, corresponding to John 4:9. That "the Johannine Christ puts himself at a permanent distance from the Jews" (Bultmann, *op. cit.,* p. 139, footnote 6) is not in contrast with John 4:22, but is an expression of the historical experience that Jesus was separated from the people, even though *sōtēria* (in the *sōtēr* Jesus) comes from them. What follows is taken from my article "Das Judenproblem im Lichte der Johannesapokalypse," *ThZ* 13 (1957), pp. 241–259.

Paul differentiates *ho en tō phanerō Ioudaios* and *ho en tō kryptō Ioudaios*. Moreover, while Paul associates the idea of the true Jew with fulfillment of the Law, the question of the Law no longer plays a role in the Revelation. Here it is a christological question. The true Jew, the one who is bound to God in reality, must have a ready ear for the proclamation of Christ, who speaks in the messages to the churches, who has revealed himself in the history of his people as the slain Lamb, the crucified Lord. The Revelation emphasizes in citations from Genesis 49:9 and Isaiah 11:1 that this Christ has come as the Messiah of the Jews, *ho leōn ho ek tēs phulēs Iouda, hē riza Dauid*. The refusal of this Lord and his church reveals the whole depth of the lost condition into which the Jews of Smyrna and Philadelphia have fallen. They have rebelled against God himself and have sold their honor, that of being God's chosen people, for the price of their self-assertion against the divine revelation. By this they have become Satan's synagogue. The uniqueness and greatness of their existence now discloses itself in this dreadful perversion of their divine destiny.

Thus, this Christless Judaism begins to play an ominous role in the Antichrist theme: it "blasphemes" the church of Christ. *Blasphēmein* and *blasphēmia* are in the Revelation the nature of the speech of the Antichrist and his followers.[140] As the enemy of the *ekklēsiai* and their Lord, Judaism has renounced its own mission as bearer of God's revelation.

Thus, the church and its history cannot be understood without at the same time having the people of Israel in the field of vision. This is wholly clear in chapter 12. We have already spoken of the general structure of the image, and will pursue here only the structuring of the woman and the child.

The woman is undoubtedly the mother of the Messiah. For a man who lives so deeply in the conceptual world of the Old Testament and the Palestinian-Jewish exegetical tradition as does our author, the mother of the Messiah can only be *the community of Israel*. If also the influence of astral mythology and the widespread conceptions of a queen of heaven are to be reckoned with in the

---

140 Revelation 13:1, 5, 6; 16:9, 11, 21; 17:3. On the concept, see W. Beyer, *TWB* 1:620ff.

structuring of the image in the vision,[141] it ought not be forgotten that already in the Jewish apocalyptic tradition the representation of Israel in the image of a woman was current, and the sun, moon, and stars had been put in connection with the people of God.[142] Consequently, the mother of the Messiah with the twelve-star crown will be the twelve-tribe people, i.e., the community of the Old Covenant.

For the Christian apocalyptist, this means that he sees the Messiah's mother experiencing a special history in connection with the historical Christ event. First of all, her place of residence is changed. At the beginning she lives in heaven, after the birth she lives on earth—somewhere—and after that in the desert. The first is quite understandable on the basis of Jewish conceptions: the Seer views the godly righteous who live with God in heaven. "I saw his dwelling under the wings of the lord of spirits. All the righteous and the elect sparkle before him like firelight, his mouth is full of benedictions" (Enoch 39:6f.).[143] And yet there is to be observed the great distinction from the Jewish tradition. The Christian apocalyptist cannot yet extol the glory and joy of the godly in heaven (even though he describes their brightness)—he sees them much more as the church which suffers and waits during the messianic birth pains.

But now how is it to be explained, that the further history of the Messiah's mother takes place on earth? In my opinion, most interpreters rashly seize on a simplification of the matter when

---

141 P. Touilleux, *op. cit.*, pp. 118–131.

142 Genesis 37:9; Testament of Naphtali 5:3ff.; Hebrew Testament of Naphtali 2–3. Cf. Judges 5:31, which with Song of Solomon 6:10; Daniel 12:3, and Deuteronomy 11:21, is frequently used in the Jewish literature to designate the glory of the departed pious (Strack and Billerbeck, *op. cit.*, III:1138ff.). A. Feuillet considers the Song of Solomon as the key saying (*Recherche de Science Religieuse* 49 [1961], pp. 321–353, and *RB* [1959], pp. 54–86).

143 Cf. 2 Esdras 14:9; perhaps also 7:28 and 13:52 (yet here one should rather think of an angel, with Gunkel, using Kautzsch's translation); Enoch 38:1: "then will the congregation of the righteous become visible [from heaven]"; according to 40:5, "the chosen of the lord of spirits are preserved"; in 70:1-4, Enoch is raised to the Son of Man in heaven, where he sees "the patriarchs and the righteous, who have dwelt in that place from time immemorial." "The chosen one already has a community about himself in heaven in the present" (Volz, *op. cit.*, p. 205); cf. also Gressmann, *Der Ursprung der israelitisch-jüdischen Eschatologie*, p. 358, and Strack and Billerbeck, *op. cit.*, IV:1143.

they identify the mother with the Christian church.[144] It will be better to get a grip on the identity of this person before and after the birth.[145] The story of Israel's godly now continues on earth, and that means, in the view of the apocalyptist, the story of the true Jews who believe in Christ—a thought which means a great deal to the Seer, as we have seen. Through this understanding the other details will also arrange themselves into a meaningful whole. In this manner the protection motif, which plays a role in the portrayal of the Messiah's mother but not with her other children, obtains its relevance. The desert, which is the place of the final election of Israel in the Jewish eschatology in connection with Hosea 2:14 and 13:5, becomes an image of the God-given place of protection for the faithful remnant of Israel.[146]

This enables us to explain a final controversial problem in chapter 12. Because the dragon cannot catch the woman, he attacks the other children of the mother of the Messiah. Who are these *loipoi tou spermatos autēs* who keep God's commandments and maintain their testimony of Jesus? There have been frequent efforts to understand the relation of the Messiah's mother and her children as representing either the relationship of the idea to the reality of the church or as the relationship of Wisdom to her pious children. This interpretation however is prohibited by the Seer's understanding of the woman as the congregation of Israel living with her children on earth. The genealogical relationship between the children and their mother as well as that between the Messiah

---

144 Catholic exegetes are also more frequently giving up any reference to Mary; cf. the survey by P. Prigent, *op. cit.,* pp. 138–140; J. Michl, "Die Deutungen der apokalyptischen Frau in der Gegenwart," *BZ* 3 (1959), pp. 301–310; A. Trabucco, "La donna ravvolta di sole, L'inerpretazione ecclesiologica degli esegeti cattolici dal 1563 alla prima metà del secolo XIX," *Marianum* 19 (1957), pp. 1–58, 289–334. Mary as a type or mother of the church is still bound with the ecclesiological exposition of B. J. Le Frois, "The Mary-Church Relationship in the Apocalypse," *Marian Studies* 92 (1958), pp. 79–106, and A. Roets, *op. cit.,* pp. 332–360.

145 This has also been maintained, rightly, by S. Giet, *op. cit.,* pp. 110f.

146 On the problem of the desert in the New Testament see W. Schmauch, *In der Wüste. Beobachtungen zur Raumbeziehung des Glaubens im NT: In Memoriam E. Lohmeyer* (1951), pp. 202–223, and the literature cited there. The movement in the desert according to Isaiah 40:3 also has eschatological significance for the Qumran community, cf. 1QS 8:12-14 (cf. Mark 1:2); 1QM 1:2-3. The desert is (among other meanings) for the Qumran community the place in which the "penitent of the desert" are kept by God (4QpPs 37 on Ps. 37:19): "Its meaning is that He will keep them alive during famine and at that time (. . .) will perish from famine and pestilence all who are not remo(ved by . . .)." The wings of the great eagle draw attention to the Old Testament (Exod. 19:4; Deut. 32:10f.; Isa. 40:31).

and his mother is rather to be explained with respect to the specific significance and function of the Jewish Christians (as well as the Gentile Christians) in the life of the church until the Parousia. To recognize these relations is an essential part of John's understanding of the church. This conception is similar to that of Paul. It has to be recalled however that this church, though differentiated in the described way, is only one indivisible congregation. To the *ekklēsiai* belong the true Jews and the Gentiles, both of whom bear witness to the continuity of the saving activity of God. For the congregation as a whole is the heir of the ancient Israel, namely, the royal priesthood of Exodus 19:6 (Rev. 1:6; 5:10), the people of the saints (Dan. 7:21), against whom the Antichrist is fighting (13:7), the true people of the twelve tribes (the 144,000 sealed: 7:1-8; 14:1-5).

This whole problem of the Jewish destiny comes yet again to expression in the impressive visions of the eleventh chapter, which we shall now discuss with necessary brevity. In two peculiarly dazzling scenes, the fate of the city of God in the End time is here portrayed.

The Seer is to *measure* "the temple of God and the altar and those who worship there" with a staff. The outer court of the temple area remains outside the space marked out. That means that it is to be surrendered to the heathen nations, like the entire holy city. The nations will trample the city with their feet for forty-two months, i.e., desecrate it. But now, during this whole time of the heathens, *two witnesses* will appear in the city, who will deliver their prophetic message in the clothing of the preachers of repentance. "These are the two olive trees and the two lampstands which stand before the Lord of the earth. And if any one would harm them, fire pours from their mouth and consumes their foes . . ." They will thus execute signs of judgment and remain unconquerable until their time is fulfilled. "They have power to shut the sky, that no rain may fall during the days of their prophesying, and they have power over the waters to turn them into blood, and to smite the earth with every plague, as often as they desire." Thus their judgmental power is portrayed in words taken from the Elijah and Moses traditions.

Both images, the image of the temple and the image of the witnesses, are indissolubly tied together by having the same time and place of action. What kind of thinking stands behind this strange metaphorical language?

Of primary interest for our exposition is the strong anchoring of the whole vision in the holy temple-city of Jerusalem. The assumption, defended by many exegetes until most recent times, that the Seer is not thinking of Jerusalem but of Rome,[147] runs afoul of the reference to the city's history in verse 8: "where their Lord was crucified," as well of the counting of the number of residents, which vaguely agrees with the number in the Jerusalem of the first century, but not with those in Rome.[148] Thus chapter 11 concerns, in a special manner, the geographical and spiritual center of Judaism, which in Jewish apocalyptic also stands in the middle of all the eschatological hopes.

a) Behind the first scene, the *measuring of the temple,* Wellhausen, as is well known, surmised the existence of a Zealot pamphlet from the time of the Roman siege which declared the hope, the temple and inner court being in the greatest peril at the moment, that the enemy attack could be defied.[149] Wellhausen's hypothesis has, in the later course of exposition, been modified in many ways. But it contributes nothing to the understanding of the whole image, for there is simply nothing here about the characteristics of the temple structure. It is to be particularly observed that the expression "measure the temple of God and the altar and those who worship there" certainly does not refer to the physical space, but only to the community characterized by the space, as similar phrases show: *hē gē kai hoi en autē katoikountes,* 13:12; *ouranoi kai hoi en autois skēnountes,* 12:12. Even here is neither earth nor heaven; only their residents are in view. This then means that all spatial ideas which are mentioned in connection with the meas-

---

147 Cf. M. Boismard, *op. cit., ad loc.,* Joh. Munck, *op. cit.* There is no kind of pause between verses 2 and 3; any introductory formula for a new vision is lacking. To eliminate 11:8 is too violent.

148 J. Jeremias, *Jerusalem zur Zeit Jesu,* reckons with 55,000 (I:96), in the Supplement, pp. 98f., with only 25–30,000 inhabitants. But Revelation 11 speaks of not even a tenth part of the inhabitants. Nevertheless, the proportions fit only Jerusalem.

149. J. Wellhausen, *Skizzen und Vorarbeiten,* 6 (1899), pp. 221ff.

urement (the outer court and the city) are to be referred to men.[150] They are to be understood metaphorically, but they ought not be dissociated from their anchoring in the concrete, historical place, the earthly sanctuary of the Jews.[151] It concerns the community which is characterized by its worship in the Jerusalem sanctuary, God's people, *Israel*. For the duration of the End time, the forty-two months or the Danielic 3½ times, the apocalyptist accordingly sees Israel split in two. One holy kernel of the temple people stand under the divine protection; the other, greater part is however surrendered to the nations to be desecrated.[152] This abandoned Jerusalem is the type of the Judaism which had crucified its Lord and thereby desecrated itself. The mention of the cross in verse 8 gives the theological evaluation of this Judaism the final proof.[153] This Jerusalem is therefore seen pneumatically:[154] Sodom and Egypt, the types of the godless and the enemies of God's people in the Old Testament. Yes, Jerusalem has now become the spiritual sister city to the great harlot Babylon, can be termed like that one, *hē polis hē megalē*, and is the sphere of power and finally the place of revelation of the beast, the Antichrist who kills the prophets of God.[155]

But for the Revelation the theme of Judaism is not thereby written off.[156] The fact that this fallen Jerusalem is deemed worthy of special attention by God until the End should warn us against such a false conclusion as drawn by many interpreters. God sends his two witnesses, both of whom are to continue speaking, thus not

---

150 A. Feuillet rightly points to the fact that even the command *ekbale* cannot be referred to the temple grounds, but only to men. He compares Matthew 8:12 and other passages (*NTS* 4 [1958] pp. 184–186). Cf. Isaiah 1:10, 12.

151 Nothing in the text suggests a reference to the church.

152 So also, with good grounds, A. Feuillet, *op. cit.*, p. 187.

153 The text says nothing at all about the destruction of the temple. Hence chapter 11 offers no hint concerning the time of writing.

154 That is, "perceived with prophetic eyes" (Ed. Schweizer, *TWB* 6:448).

155 Cf. Isaiah 1:9f.; Ezekiel 16:46, 49. Egypt plays the role of the heathenish world power in the Old Testament in a distinctive way (see also Wisdom of Solomon 19:14f.). The name of a country can be used for a city, for the city in the Old Testament is often the symbol and content of the nation. That these designations should harmonize with Rome better than with Jerusalem is baffling, seeing that in the Old Testament Egypt is not used to refer also to Jerusalem and Israel (against Joh. Munck, *op. cit.*, pp. 34f.). Cf. also G. Schrenk, *Die Weissagung über Israel im Neuen Testament* (1951), pp. 41f.

156 Inconceivable, for instance, to Ed. Meyer, *Ursprung und Anfänge des Christentums*, Vol. 2 (1921), p. 381: "The Jews are for him as fully done with as for the Gospel of John."

leaving this Jerusalem finally without his message and freeing it from its special responsibility. This divine message, however, issues no longer from the mouth of this rejected Judaism. *Vocem quam habebat, amiserit . . . mutus ergo populus sine ratione, sine verbo,* as Ambrosius paraphrases the Jewish situation in his commentary on Luke.[157]

Israel thus retains its special character among the nations. It is indeed put into the background for a definite time and trampled, but yet it is not disintegrated or annihilated. It becomes the synagogue of Satan, but it remains in association with the God who chose it. It is mixed among the nations, but yet it cannot be assimilated and lose its special appearance. It no longer bears the life-giving word of God to all nations and times, but the fatal silence of God. This is the mystery of its further history. The fact that it is not extinguished, but only placed in the shadow, remains an open question for the future, to the end of all the history of this aeon.

b) That is the one aspect of the Jewish problem in the Revelation; the other is encountered in the image of that Judaism which is not surrendered to the nations. It is, in truth, temple and altar, the multitude of true worshipers (11:1). This saying really leads very near to the Gospel of John, which speaks of the true worshipers in spirit and truth (John 4:21-24). This latter utterance is meant, however, to be universal, while the Revelation speaks of worshipers from the temple people, that is, out of that Judaism which has not resisted the revelation of the Lord on the cross. Therefore they are not desecrated, not made like the nations. They are *the true Jews,* who bear this name of honor rightfully—in contrast to the Judaism found in Smyrna and Philadelphia. Thus to the Seer, the existence of a Judaism which believes in Christ appears to correspond to a divine necessity. He is thereby brought very close to the Apostle Paul, who recognizes the existence of Jewish Christians within the church as proof of the divine faithfulness to his people and to his promises (Rom. 9–11).

It is on the basis of the foregoing that I believe that we have to

---

157 Migne, *Ser. lat.* XV, 1550.

understand the second part of the Jerusalem vision of chapter 11 (11:3-14). This second image portrays the time of the heathens begun by the schism of Israel, the time before the End, designated with numbers taken from Daniel. The number of the months here is not chosen accidentally, for the same number is used in the thirteenth chapter for the Antichrist's period of rule. The heathen are instruments of the Antichrist. It is this same time span which is granted to the two witnesses for their proclamation, 1260 days. The number of days is in the twelfth chapter the time of the protection for the woman in the desert, which again points to a specific connection. This whole time is portrayed here with a certain narrowing of the field of view toward Jerusalem.[158]

The two *witness figures* are brought together with several traditions from the Old Testament.[159] Like Elijah and Moses, they are witnesses of the divine authority.[160] They are at the same time the two olive trees of Zechariah 4. In one of his night visions Zechariah sees a lampstand all of gold, "and there are two olive trees by it, one on the right of the bowl and the other on its left." The olive trees are interpreted: "These are the two anointed who stand by the Lord of the whole earth." Following the rabbinic interpretation of this passage of Zechariah, the priestly and kingly function of the witnesses is in mind.[161] The Revelation departs from Zechariah insofar as it speaks of only one lampstand; here however, the two witnesses are called *hai duo luchniai*. They have a message to direct to Jerusalem which is characterized as a message of repentance and is accompanied by signs of judgment.[162] For Israel in its unbelief God has no other word than the word which calls Israel back to its proper destiny.

---

158 Jerusalem-Israel is plainly a type of the fate of the world. Hence the many nations of 11:9f.

159 There is no genuine connection with the Jewish conception of the messianic forerunners, for according to 11:8, the Messiah has already come—apart from the question of whether a tradition of two forerunners is at all detectable; cf. J. Jeremias, *TWB* 2:941ff.; J. Munck, *op. cit.*, pp. 81–120.

160 1 Kings 17:1; Exodus 7:17, 19. Similar statements are made in connection with the prayers of the saints in Revelation 8:3-6.

161 Cf. Strack and Billerbeck, *op. cit.*, III:811f. Cf. p. 87.

162 Cf. Jeremiah 5:14: "I am making my words in your mouth a fire." We can cite here also the primitive Christian traditions about the power of the Spirit-filled words: Matthew 10:14f.; 16:19; 18:18; Acts 5:5, 10; 12:23; 13:11ff.; Luke 10:13–16. Behind the word of the church stands the Lord himself.

What now does the Seer understand by these two witnesses? That is nowhere said *expressis verbis,* so that we are driven to undertake it on the basis of the rest of the image material of the Revelation—if this is really possible—and so derive an interpretation. It strikes us immediately that the two witnesses bear no individualized traits—they are not even simply identified with Elijah and Moses—and that they exceed all individual human bounds. Hence they appear at best, like many other images of the Revelation, to be conceived as images of a collective idea. We can go even further in a certain direction: many details used to characterize the two witnesses connect them with various statements of the book concerning the Christian church, so that the interpretation of the two witnesses makes plain reference to *the church in Jerusalem.*

The following associated details are interesting in this connection.

The function of the two figures is defined as "witnesses." Their whole life is God's message. This brings to mind the designation of Jesus: *martys* (1:5; 3:14), and the members of his church (2:13; 17:6) who maintain the *martyria Iēsou* (6:9; 12:11, 17; 19:10; 20:4).[163] The naming of the witnesses as "lampstands" suggests the introductory vision in which the churches encircle Christ like seven lampstands. Add to this that the apocalyptist likes to transfer the office of king and priest, which is intimated in the Zechariah citation, to the church of Christ. All this points in the same direction: the witnesses are an image of the church.[164] Only the doubling of the witnesses is problematical. It may be that it already lay at hand in traditional conceptions. But what has the

---

163 Whether *martys* really designates martyrs and only the evangelistically-prophetically active martyrs (so Holtz, *op. cit.,* pp. 55f.) is uncertain at least. Not 1:5 or 3:14 or even 11:3 binds death absolutely with the idea of witness, but rather with the prophetic office! Certainly, however, as also in 2:13 and 17:6, martyrdom is a consequence of the "witnessing" service.

164 The expression *ho kyrios autōn* in 11:8, which is quite unique in the New Testament, speaks on behalf of this. Holtz draws attention to the oddness of the passage, with this justified conclusion: Christ in the New Testament is "not the Lord of particular men but the Lord of the church or Lord of the world." Therefore he is thinking here not primarily of the title "Kyrios," but considers it to be an expression of Jesus' ruling relationship to the two witnesses. But there is no good reason for this opinion, as the lord-servant relationship plays no role in 11:3–13. Corresponding to the common primitive Christian expression *ho kyrios hēmōn* which Paul often uses, Christ is here called the Kyrios of the witnesses, i.e., even of the church.

Seer involved in this? The doubling in the image of the church receives its good sense when we think of the special theme of chapter 11. It certainly concerns Israel, whose Christ-believing part has a special salvation history meaning, as the image of the true worshipers has already shown. It is not going too far to see this Christ-believing Israel set forth in one of the two witnesses, next to whom appears the other witness, the witness out of the Gentile world, that is, the host of the heathens, who are by the blood of the Lamb ransomed "for God from every tribe and tongue and people and nation, and . . . made . . . a kingdom and priests to our God," as the hymn of 5:9f. celebrates. Together they constitute the one congregation of Jerusalem. Therefore they are placed side by side without any individual distinctions. They speak and do the same thing at the same time. And yet this duality in their unity is important for the apocalyptist, for in it is contained the meaning of Jewish existence in the present. We again call to mind this same historical-theological thinking, which the Apostle Paul develops in Romans.

In this way an inner connection in the two images of the eleventh chapter has now become visible, a connection which reaches out over the geographical and temporal unity: the whole vision speaks of the mystery of Israel, which is inseparably bound up with the Christian church.

With the conclusion of the End time the duty of the witnesses is also accomplished. Then the beast from the bottomless pit, the Antichrist, conquers them and kills them. Afterward their bodies lie unburied for 3½ days in the street, to the joy of those who dwell on earth, and the church thus is deeply humiliated.[165] Then there is done for the witnesses the miracle of awakening to new life, according to Ezekiel 37:5, 10.[166] Joh. Munck has rightly drawn attention to the uniqueness of this account of the awakening, which has no parallels in the New Testament's resurrection and ascension

---

165 3½ days marks, in contrast to the whole End time (3½ times), the brevity of the final period of most extreme tribulation. The "broken sevenfold," which has no full duration, can possibly be brought into relationship with Matthew 24:22 also.

166 The resurrection is also described in Revelation 20:4f. with this same Old Testament expression.

stories.[167] They are certainly sought there in the wrong place, for the individual resurrection of single people is not involved here, rather, the inclusive eschatological event which is associated with the Parousia. The nearest parallel is offered by the account of the taking up of the church at the Parousia in 1 Thessalonians 4:16f. The correspondences are clear:

"Then they heard a loud voice from heaven" (vs. 12).

"For the Lord himself will descend from heaven with a cry of command, with the archangel's call" (1 Thess. 4:16).

"They went up to heaven in a cloud" (vs. 12).

"We . . . shall be caught up . . . in the clouds to meet the Lord in the air" (1 Thess. 4:17).[168]

Revelation 11:11-13 thus portrays the taking up of the church to be with the Lord. A great earthquake introduces the destruction of the old world (cf. 6:12; 16:18), destroys a tenth part of the city, kills seven thousand people, and leads to terror and the giving of glory to God.[169]

Finally, we have yet to outline the duty of the church according to the Revelation. As the people of God, the true community of the Old Testament and the church of Christ have to be bearers of witness (11:1-13), for only in their witness is salvation, the victory, to be found. Therefore the church is seen as the multitude of witnesses and as the lampstand which illuminates the world. The church carries out its priestly service as bearer of the word (1:6; 5:10; 20:6). Thus the church lives not only by God's gracious appeal, but is itself the bearer of this call to all the peoples. In this way the church becomes the final destiny of the nations.

It is significant, therefore, that the angel follows the radiant image of the chosen ones of the Lamb on Zion, the angel who proclaims as the word of God for those who dwell on earth of all nations not judgment, but "an eternal gospel," calling men to the worship of God (14:6-7)! The two angels following him certainly point to the

---

167 Munck, *op. cit.,* p. 42.

168 The clouds belong to the Parousia traditions, after Daniel 7:13; cf. Revelation 1:7; 14:14; Mark 13:26 and parallels; Acts 1:9, 11.

169 To find Israel's conversion prophesied here will not do; the Seer is thinking of men from all nations (11:9). Rather, there is depicted here the positive aspect of the unavoidable recognition of the final hour, while 6:15f. speaks only of the reaction of anguish.

gravity of this offer of grace and warn against the desperate attempt (still so attractive appearing within general history) to side with powerful Babylon and the beast. God's victory, which permits the proclamation of his gospel to the world, is irresistible, and all attempts to live by oneself, to renounce the grace of the Lamb, will be quickly unmasked and judged as demonic efforts.

It becomes clearly apparent in this passage that John does not intend to give a complete presentation of the End time in the sense of a determined history of calamity and judgment, as the series of sevenfold visionary images might easily permit. Rather, he has in mind here a power which can break open all the uniformity of history.

All the visions of judgment, which stand under the divine "must," have finally a very evident "if not" before them. So long as the world despises the gospel, the gracious word will turn into a word of judgment. In this, John distinguishes himself basically from the historical images of Jewish apocalyptic, for which history constitutes a determinate, inclusive unity.[170] The church is the priestly sign of this openness of history, the sign of the promise of grace for all men.[171]

4. DEATH IN THE END TIME

The personal destiny of the individual is in the Revelation fully tied in with the result of the whole of salvation's history. Although the time of messianic salvation has already broken in, the powers of Antichrist yet rule over the earth. These are first conquered covertly, by faith. A particular expression of this situation is the still enduring visible omnipotence of death.

Death is seen in the Revelation, as in the whole Bible, as one of the powers at enmity with God. It is one of the riders in the train

---

170 D. Rössler, *op. cit.*, pp. 55ff.
171 In 14:14, *aparchē* scarcely means simply "votive offering"; it means rather "first-born" (cf. Rom. 8:23; 11:16; 1 Cor. 16:15; 15:20, 23) and designates the church as a promise for all men. The association of the idea of the *aparchē* with these *anthrōpoi* forbids the assumption of any sort of sequence from the first to the later Christian generations (Hadorn), or from an elite to the whole group of the redeemed (Allo and others). That it does not concern the contrast of Jew to Gentile (Spitta, Zahn, and others) follows from the definition of the 144,000.

of the Antichrist (6:8[172]) and is thrown into the lake of fire at the End (20:14). Its companion, Hades, is also understood as a person (1:18; 6:8; 20:13f.). Hades is not only thought of as the general place of the dead or its ruler, but as the place of the wretched and their ruler. The idea of Hades corresponds to an older type of Sheol conception in Judaism, which no longer saw in it only the general place of the dead—but neither did it see in it the place of final eschatological damnation.[173] The apocalyptist is thus aware of an individual, immediate sentence after death, which however is not yet final.[174]

But now the Revelation allows the light of God's new revelation in the redemptive act of Jesus Christ to shine also into this dark sphere of the greatest danger to the messianic lordship of Jesus. The End time is even introduced by the eschatological event of the conquering of death in the resurrection of Jesus (see 1:5, 18). As victor over death, Jesus Christ also rules over Hades: "I have the keys of Death and Hades" (1:18).[175]

Jesus Christ enables men to guard against Hades, for with the

---

172 1:18; 6:8; 20:13f., clearly portray death as a demonic person. Only in 21:4, where the ruler of Hades is not mentioned at the same time (cf. J. Jeremias, *TWB* 3:746), does *ho thanatos* mean "death," for it stands here in a series with the wholly impersonal ideas of "tears, mourning, crying, and pain." In 20:13, the ideas of "Death and Hades" carry a spatial sense (cf. W. Bieder, *Die Vorstellung von der Höllenfahrt Jesu Christi, ATANT*, Vol. 19 [1949], p. 94); "in them" moreover does not speak decisively against recognizing that the preponderant idea here, as in the immediately following verse 14, is of a personal nature. For (as in the Old Testament), one cannot make a hard and fast distinction between death's aspect of personal power and that of location. "Death and the realm of death as personal powers are used promiscuously [in the Old Testament]" (Chr. Barth, *Die Errettung vom Tode* [1947], pp. 76, 89). On the ocean as the place of death's realm (20:13), cf. Barth, *op. cit.*, pp. 85f., and Ph. Reymond, *op. cit.*, pp. 212–214.

173 Cf. perhaps Enoch 22; Ezra 7:25ff.; Apocalypse of Baruch 36:10f. The statements of late Judaism are not uniform on this point, the older conceptions standing near the later. Cf. J. Jeremias, *Weltvollender*, p. 63; E. Stauffer, *op. cit.*, § 52, and Strack and Billerbeck, *op. cit.*, IV:1017ff.; Volz, *op. cit.*, § 38, and H. Bietenhard, "Kennt das NT die Vorstellung vom Fegfeuer," *ThZ* 3 (1947), pp. 101ff.

174 So also Luke 16:22ff.; Acts 1:25; 1 Peter 3:19; 4:6. Cf. Ad. Schlatter, *Die Theologie des NT* (1909–1910), Vol. I, pp. 222f., and especially O. Cullmann, *Immortality of the Soul or Resurrection of the Dead?* (1959), Chapter 4.

175 Death and Hades are thought of as persons here also, as is the case wherever they occur together in the Revelation. Thus the genetive can only be understood as a possessive. The image of the key, which is also used in the rabbinic writings for God's power over death (cf. Jerusalem Targum II on Gen. 30:22 and Deut. 28:12; Sanhedrin 113a; Ta'anith 2a), stands here in connection with the conception of Christ's descent into Hades, yet this has no constitutive meaning for this passage. It is simply maintained that Christ disposes of the destiny of men in the intermediary time not only during their life on earth but also in death. Cf. W. Bieder, *op. cit.*, pp. 92–96; J. Jeremias, *ZNW* 42 (1949), pp. 194–201.

resurrected one "Life" has entered into the passing world and its orders. Thus, in 21:6, the gift of salvation promises the eschatological $z\bar{o}\bar{e}$ for the present.[176] This eschatological life from the world of God (cf. 2:7, 10; 7:17; 22:2, 14, 19) is not achieved first in death or by the resurrection, but in the present moment of the intermediary time. Yet the church has life only in its association with Christ, never in itself alone. Thus a warning must be sent to the church of Sardis, which has the name of being alive, and yet is dead (3:1). One can be "blotted out" from the book of life (3:5), which is the Lamb's book (13:8).

Life is mediated by the Spirit, which is the same as the breath of life (11:11; cf. Ezek. 37:9f.). This is probably the basis on which John, in the message to the church at Sardis, which lacks life, sees in the hand of Christ not only the seven stars, but, in addition, the seven spirits, the fullness of the Holy Spirit.[177]

In the Johannine manner the Spirit is also designated as living water, which is given to those who thirst[178] (21:6; 22:17). Accordingly, for these two passages a similar double meaning is yielded as for 3:20: the immediate presence of the gift is in mind, yet at the same time its futurity. For the present share in life does not make the future consummation superfluous, but directly promises it.

I have remarked on the nearness of the Revelation to John's Gospel. They are certainly to be distinguished in that the Revelation, above all, speaks of the *consummation* of the life which is now present, while the Gospel proclaims the *presence* of the life which will be fulfilled in the future. For the Gospel and the Revelation, however, the Christ event is primarily recognizable as a new creation for faith;[179] all the riddles and consequences of sin remain in

---

176 $Z\bar{o}\bar{e}$ in association with $hyd\bar{o}r$ stands in connection with the water of Paradise (cf. Rev. 22:1; Gen. 2:10–14; Ezek. 47:1, 7; Zech. 14:8; Joel 3:18). On the idea of the water of life, cf. John 4:1–42; 7:37–39 (cf. Bultmann, *Das Johannesevangelium*, pp. 133–136, and Bauer, *op. cit.*, excursus on John 4:1, pp. 68f.). Cf. J. Jeremias, *Weltvollender*, pp. 45–52, and Ph. Reymond, *op. cit.*, pp. 234–244.

177 Paul is also thinking of the gift of the Spirit when he speaks of the condition of nakedness during the waiting period after death in 2 Corinthians 5:1–10.

178 The similarity to John 7:37–39 is unmistakable. Lohmeyer is far off the point when he refers to the "not-yet-martyrs" whose "faith is yet to be consummated in death" (*op. cit.*, p. 165).

179 Cf. the emphasizing of faith in John 3:18 and 1:13.

continued existence for the cosmos.[180] Basically, we may hold for
the Johannine eschatology, fully corresponding to that of the Revelation, what Schniewind[181] writes: "The greatness of the Johannine
statement becomes clear only from the radical questioning which
is acquainted with the passing away of heaven and earth, . . . of
our world." The cosmic direction of eschatological thinking is also
preserved throughout in John's Gospel. But the character of the
intermediary present time, defined by the event of Jesus Christ as
the central occurrence of salvation history, and in which the final
eschatological crisis occurs (cf. John 3:17-21, 36) through the encounter with the message of Jesus Christ (and hence with him himself), is emphasized in an extraordinarily strong manner. But this
does not create an abyss between those statements which call
attention to the reality and presence of salvation in the faith in Jesus
Christ and those which maintain the thought of future consummation. To the contrary, one can acquire a different view only by doing
violence to the text, by wholly arbitrary deletions.[182] The Revelation shows the same state of affairs as John's Gospel, setting forth
metaphorically the crisis which occurred in the past and is self-
consummating in the encounter with the Lord of the church. The
figure used is that of the Son of Man, who brings down the final
judgment as the Lord of the church in the intermediary time, who
is the eschatological judge and out of whose mouth the word of
judgment now issues (1:12-16). By the same figure of the Son of
Man with the word of judgment, Christ is also designated as the
future judge (19:15). Even the final judgment (20:11-15) reveals
and makes real only the decision already made. Its criterion is that
of being written in the Lamb's book of life (20:15).

This openly exhibited situation of the church in the intermediary
time exists also for the dead. Salvation's now-present gift of life
is effectual even in the midst of death. This life cannot be lost.
Those sealed cannot be brought to ruin (cf. John 11:25f.) by the

---

180 God's love for the world (John 3:16) comes to its goal primarily in the consummation which is understood as a future event: John 5:28f.; 6:39, 44, 54; 10:16;
11:24f.; 12:32, 48; 14:3; 15:6; 17:24; 21:22.

181 In *Kerygma and Myth*, p. 81f.

182 E. Stählin, *ZNW* 31 (1934), p. 237, has previously noted, correctly: "Had the
interpolator intended to insert his own, i.e., the customary, eschatological conceptions,
he would have been acting with unbelievable ineptitude."

eschatological events, to which the efficacy of death also properly belongs (Rcv. 6:8), nor can they be separated from their Lord, whose name they bear (Rom. 8:38f.).[183]

The efficacy of Christ's act even over death is especially emphasized in 14:13. Since the Christ event[184] there has been a dying *en kyriō*. There is no need to think of this as a martyrdom.[185] The expression is best explained by analogy to 1 Corinthians 15:18 and 1 Thessalonians 4:16: "sharing in the Lord" remains inviolate even in death. Hence the believing dead are called *makarioi*, they have left their labors behind them,[186] and their "deeds" follow them.[187] The "following" of the deeds is intended to demonstrate their value before God. They are *peplērōmena* (3:2; cf. similarly 1 Corinthians 15:58). And it is not unimportant that in 14:13 the Spirit is introduced as speaking. This reiterates the connection of the "dead in the Lord" with the Spirit and life.

This effectuality of life over death is seen in three great scenes in the Revelation, as a promise and a strengthening for all who must die before the *kairos* (1:3).

Previously, in 12:1, there has come to us the image of the faithful dead of the time prior to Christ.[188] In contrast to the portrayal of those who die after the Christ event, here the suffering and fear involved in hope are strongly emphasized. They still stand in the messianic birth pangs.

In 6:9-11, the Revelation shows an initial group of those who have died in the Lord and are indeed martyrs (cf. 6:9: *tōn esphagmenōn*). They are seen under the heavenly altar; that is, in the "unmediated presence of God."[189] They wear the white robes

---

183 Cf. John 10:28. See O. Cullmann, *op. cit.*, chapter 4.

184 Cf. pp. 35ff.

185 One obstructs the general understanding of the Revelation if he sees in it, one-sidedly, *only* a book of martyrs.

186 14:13b; the *kopoi* are to be understood as synonymous with *thlipsis* (cf. 7:9ff.).

187 The "following" of the deeds "includes the thought that these works will exist before God in the final judgment, when all godless works are destroyed"; cf. Greek Enoch 97:6 (J. Jeremias, *ZNW* [1939], p. 123).

188 Cf. pp. 93ff.

189 Heaven as a temple, also in 11:19; 15:5; cf. Exodus 25:9, 40; 26:30; 27:8. Revelation very probably distinguished two heavenly altars. One is the golden altar of incense offerings (8:3; 9:13; cf. Exod. 30:3). The other altar is not called golden, but is strikingly associated with God's presence (14:15, 18; 16:17) and brought into connection with the conception in 6:9, for in 16:7 a voice from the altar confirms and praises the truth and righteousness of God's judgments over his enemies, who "have shed the

of the heavenly.[190] But their consummation is not yet accomplished; they yet await the final revelation of God's honor in judgment (6:10).

The resurrection of the martyrs is first spoken of in the context of the millennial hope (20:4). Nothing is stated about the manner of existence of the dead.[191] The *psychē* type of existence of the dead still belongs to this world era prior to the Parousia and the resurrection. The existence of the dead is still characterized by the great waiting (6:11), in which they—together with those who live in the intermediary time—stand.

John sees the second scene in 7:9-17. The 144,000 stand as an image of the whole church of the End time as over against the uncountable host of the redeemed in heaven. They wear the white robes of the heavenly, the gracious gift of the Lamb offered for them ("washed . . . in the blood of the Lamb," 7:14), and bear palms in their hands as signs of victory (cf. 1 Macc. 13:51; 2 Macc. 10:7). They are already withdrawn from the great tribulation which belongs to the Christian existence of the End time (1:6, 9; martyrs are not in mind). Their duties consist of heavenly worship. They are not yet in the renewed world of the consummation, as it is portrayed in 21:1–22:5, and yet they already are serving before God's throne and have a share in the comforts of the future (7:15b-17).

It is thus the same church, seen as the embattled church on

---

blood of saints and prophets" (16:6). Behind the conception of the martyrs under the heavenly altar stand Old Testament (Lev. 4:7; 17:11) and Jewish ideas (Aboth RN 26 [cf. Strack and Billerbeck, *op. cit.*, I:224f.]). On the idea of the martyr as an offering to God, cf. also Philippians 2:17; 2 Timothy 4:6; Ignatius to the Romans 2:2. A place of special glory in heaven is also promised the martyrs in the Apostolic Fathers (cf. I Clement 5:4, 7; II Clement 1:2; Barnabas 19:1; Ignatius to the Magnesians 5:1; Shepherd of Hermas, Vision III, 5:5; 7:5, 6; Similitude V, 6:7; IX, 27:3). Joh. Munck's discussion (*op. cit.*, pp. 75–77), which would make use of I Clement 5:4 for his thesis of the ascension of the two apostles, cannot shake the exegesis of Knopf, *Hdb. L.*, Supplementary Vol. I (1920). Only the apocryphal Acts of the Apostles speaks of appearances of the apostles. The transition from there to I Clement and Revelation 11 is too great to allow one to discover any connecting link.

190 Lohmeyer, *op. cit.*, *ad loc.* Cf. the indices to the Mandaean literature; Ethiopian Enoch 62:15; Slavonic Enoch 22:8; Mark 9:3; 16:5; Acts 1:10 (cf. Gressmann, *op. cit.*, pp. 345f.; Volz, *op. cit.*, p. 398; Bousset, *Die Religion des Judentums*, pp. 277f.; Oepke, *TWB* 4:25–27, 251).

191 The psyche-concept keeps its Old Testament definition, it can be interpreted as "living, vital energy" (8:9; 12:11; 16:3); the soul is the seat of the appetites (18:14), interpreted as "slaves" (18:13; Ezek. 27:13).

earth in 7:1-8, after its entry into heaven. Because the Lamb has been victorious, death is no longer a horror for the church, but only a passing out of great tribulation (7:14). While in 7:1-8 their number is written down as a sign of election, now they are seen in heaven in their innumerable fullness.

A similar scene of the chosen dead is found in 15:1-4. Here is seen once again, as an insertion in the visions of the last evil time, the condition of the faithful dead. This is intended as an encouragement for those living in tribulation. The situation of the "victors" is sketched very clearly. It is impossible to have in mind here an image of the fulfilled kingdom of God, for what is set forth is placed in the midst of the preliminaries to the last plague judgment of world history. Already the sea of glass is mingled with the fire of the judgment now commencing.[192] The dead are called: *nikōntes ek tou thēriou kai ek tēs eikonos autou (kai tou arithmou tou onomatos autou)*. They are victors over the beast and his living image in the power of the Lamb (12:10f.).[193] They stand like Israel after the passage through the Red Sea in a place of safety and sing the song of Moses (the Old Testament liberator) and of the eschatological redeemer, the Lamb. The song is certainly not to be understood as a song of judgment, but as praise of the act of redemption, full of the hope of salvation for all nations.

We have thus seen that the Revelation knows individual death as arranged in the great termination of the whole of salvation history. Also, the believers are first admitted to the consummation, to the resurrection, by the Parousia. But as the resurrected one's powers of life are already given him in the intermediary time of the church on earth, so also is it given to those "dead in the Lord." After their death they stand even nearer to God than during their lifetime on earth. But death is not thereby glorified and stripped of its judgmental meaning, dying does not yet mean "coming to one's reality,"[194] but to be dead still means: nakedness, lacking the resur-

---

192 Cf. Slavonic Enoch 29:2. Cf. K. L. Schmidt, *ThZ* 3 (1947), p. 171.
193 *Nikan ek* is a Hebraism ("to be stronger than" = *min*). "The number of its name" belongs to the later additions.
194 Reisner, *op. cit.*, p. 142. Cf. also P. Althaus, *Die letzten Dinge,* 4th ed. (1933), pp. 135ff.

rection body. The believer first comes to his genuine, God-intended life in the consummated condition in the future resurrection.[195]

The saved messianic congregation, which already has a share in the blessings of eschatological salvation, includes in its scope the elect on earth and in heaven. They constitute together the great church, which waits for the appearing of the glory of God in Jesus Christ.[196]

It has become visible in what is now worked out that the Revelation, in reference to its teaching about death in the intermediary time, stands completely in line with the rest of the New Testament. Thus Jesus also speaks of an entry into heaven with death: Luke 16:22ff.; 23:43 (among purely futuristic sayings about the final judgment and the resurrection). And Paul knows what death means: to be "with Christ" (Phil. 1:23) and to be "at home with the Lord" (2 Cor. 5:8), for even he is permeated by the strong confidence which rings out again and again in John's Gospel: "He who believes in me, though he die, yet shall he live" (John 11:25).[197]

5. THE IMMINENT EXPECTATION

The Revelation shares with the whole New Testament the hope for the speedy breaking in of the End: cf. 1:3; 3:3; 16:15; 22:7, 10, 17, 20.[198]

Even so, the Seer knows that before the Parousia a series of

---

195 Cf. pp. 116ff. When P. Althaus objects against this theory of the interim situation that the decision of the last judgment would be anticipated in this way and leave no more content for that judgment (*op. cit.*, pp. 149–151), he does not observe sufficiently that life on earth already anticipates the whole decision (John 3:18!), certainly confirmed at death but initially revealed and made efficacious by the last judgment in its final consequences.

196 The earthly and the heavenly churches are perhaps seen in 13:6f. While the earthly church still suffers within range of the Antichrist's assault, the heavenly church can only be faintly slandered, for the satanic power has been thrown out of heaven (12:13). It is possible, however, that here angels are meant (cf. 1QH 3:19–23).

197 Philippians 1:21–24 can be arranged in this connection without difficulty. The exegesis of Alb. Schweitzer, *Die Mystik des Apostels Paulus* (1930), pp. 135–138, which Joh. Munck (*op. cit.*, pp. 39f.) takes up, that Paul thinks here of his own immediate resurrection after death as a special grace, is hardly possible (see M. Dibelius, in the excursis to Phil. 1:23, *op. cit.*, pp. 68–70, and on the whole passage also Eth. Stauffer, *op. cit.*, p. 186, as well as O. Cullmann, *op. cit.*, and R. Mehl, *Der letzte Feind* [1954]).

198 Cf. Mark 13:28f. and parallels; Romans 13:11f. (see the discussion by W. G. Kümmel, *Promise and Fulfilment*, pp. 19ff., 54ff.); Philippians 4:5; 1 Thessalonians 4:15; 1 Corinthians 15:51; 1 John 2:8. Cf. O. Cullmann, *Christ and Time*, I, 5; W. Michaelis, *Der Herr verzieht nicht die Verheissung.*

events will run their course, that the time between the historical Christ event and the Parousia has a special meaning for the history of salvation as the time of the hidden messianic kingdom, during which the full number of the elect are saved,[199] sinners will be called to repentance by the divine judgment (cf. 9:20f.) and the lordship of the Antichrist will come to its full extent. The duration of this intermediary time has thus always for the Seer a definite extent, for he sees a very great number of the faithful dying in the intermediary time, and the martyrs sighing over the length of the intermediary time (6:10).

The length of this period is expressed with the traditional 3½ times and indicated thereby as incalculable for men. The Seer has the conviction that the human ideas of time's dimension, by which the divine plan of salvation is reckoned, are not suitable (cf. 2 Peter 3:8).

And yet there runs throughout the whole Revelation an expectation of a speedy End, an expectation full of an enormous passion. The time is near, the delay is short (6:11; 12:12).[200] From whence comes the intensity of this imminent expectation? From our investigation, the basis is easy to define. We have seen that the Revelation bases the beginning of the End time not, like the Jewish apocalyptic, on any striking event of its own time, even though it is qualitatively, not absolutely, distinct from any others; but the time is certified by God himself, known in the appearance of the Messiah Jesus on earth.

The End, the time of messianic salvation, has already begun. This kindles the passion of the Seer's expectation. From this certainty that the last time has broken in with the historical coming of Jesus Christ and has been irrevocably introduced by God, is to be explained all the intense expectation of the New Testament.

The Seer's hope is in this way *hypomonē Iēsou,*[201] a waiting for

---

199 In 6:11, of the martyrs, and in 7:1ff. (expressed by the numbers), of the whole church.

200 An intensifying of the imminent expectation is to be recognized in the secondary interpretation of chapter 17: the time of the Antichrist is very soon to expire (17:10ff.).

201 1:9; 3:10. 1:9 is to be read with Dionysius of Alexandria (Eusebius, *Hist. Eccl.* VII, 25:11): *en hypomonē Iēsou,* which then means the same as 3:10 (*tēs hypomonēs mou*): "the steadfastness of Christ," as in 2 Thessalonians 3:5 (cf. Zahn, *op. cit.,* p. 179, also Lohmeyer, Hadorn, Behm, and others).

the appearance of Jesus; that is, for the one who has already appeared, the crucified (1:7), for him who has already decided all things for the believers. This expectation, which relies on faith in the Jesus who has come, also gives strength to the dying, because life and death have been overcome by him.

Thus the Revelation also diverges from Jewish apocalyptic in its expectation of the near End, because its hope lies grounded in the Christ event of the past and thus in his coming again.[202]

6. TIME, HISTORY, AND SALVATION

As does the Jewish apocalyptic, John associates his faith with a plan of divine action grounded in the unity and goal of history.[203] The "deputy" of God, the Lamb, brings history into movement and leads it to its goal (6:1ff.; 19:11ff.). God's plan in John's Revelation is as little a matter of an automatically running clockwork as it is in Jewish apocalyptic; it is much more a goal-directed sequence of intrusions by God into human history. But it is in the authorization of the Lamb that the deepest distinction lies in comparison with Jewish hopes. The Lamb is not only the executive power of the divine will, as are the angel figures who have also been seen acting in the Revelation, but in the Lamb—in the history of Jesus Christ, his Incarnation, his death and victory—the End, the goal of all history, is revealed already and is now at work in the realm of the believing community—for Christ is present in his church through his Spirit. But the Jewish hope of salvation remains strongly directed toward the future.[204] The future can now bring only the final disclosure and working out of Jesus' victory in every area of the world: for disbelief, a revelation of the honor and justice of God in judgment; for faith, the resurrection and salvation.

In contrast with the closed determinism in history characteristic of the Jewish apocalyptic, John gets from the overwhelming experience of the central revelation of God in Jesus an insight into

---

202 Cf. O. Cullmann, *op. cit.,* I, 5.

203 On the historical imagery of apocalyptic, cf. especially M. Noth, "Das Geschichtsverständnis der alttestamentlichen Apokalyptik" (in the omnibus *Gesammelte Studien zum Alten Testament* [1957]), pp. 248–273; O. Plöger, *Theokratie und Eschatologie* (1959); D. Rössler, *op. cit.,* pp. 58ff.

204 This is a different matter from the various visionary insights into heaven and the various individual ascensions of isolated apocalyptists.

the openness of history, the possibility of change. The church of Jesus is not, like Israel in the view of Jewish apocalyptic, simply the elect; it is at the same time a promise to all nations (the first fruits, 14:4). The initial word of God, which introduces the End, is therefore not of judgment, but is an eternal gospel to every nation (14:6f.).

The earthly bearer of the message is the church. Therefore, the whole historical event which the Revelation describes is concentrated in the question of God, a question which comes to the fore in the church and becomes decisive for world history.[205]

With the new people of God chosen out of all the nations, the national limitations of Judaism are naturally pushed to one side and the horizon of this historical view is genuinely opened up to the whole world, for the entire world is confronted with the church of Jesus.[206]

Yet another important distinction between John's Revelation and Jewish apocalyptic is to be brought to attention. John is not writing under the pseudonym of some earlier man of God. "What is" (1:19) includes his real historical present. Naturally, the Seer also looks back above all to the drama of salvation in the story of Jesus, for that is the true beginning of the End time which defines the character of the present. Thus Christ himself, or his word, now stands in the new story of salvation, in place of the apocalyptically understood Law, as the symbol of election. Just as the Law in the apocalypses, on which the decision for salvation or condemnation devolves,[207] must be "preserved,"[208] so also with the gospel in the time now understood in Christ.

And thus John does not present the generally known events of the past as self-evident fictitious prophecy, to which is then

205 To this extent, both for John and Jewish apocalyptic, "the powers and nations do not have their own history" (Rössler, op. cit., p. 64). H. Schlier, Die Zeit der Kirche (1958), p. 272, rightly refers to the grotesque proportions of this historical view: ". . . the beast of all beasts . . . at war with—a few saints! . . . The mighty cosmopolis, which is drunk—with the blood of the few witnesses to Jesus!"

206 11:9; especially emphasized in chapter 13, cf. 13:3, 7, 8, 12, 14, 16; 16:14; 17:2, 8; 18:1, 3, 9, 11.

207 Rössler, op. cit., pp. 70–77.

208 Ethiopian Enoch 108:1; 2 Esdras 7:89, 94; Syriac Baruch 44:3, 14; Rössler, op. cit., pp. 85f. The church of Jesus "preserves" not only the commandments of God, but also the testimony of Jesus (1:3; 12:11, 17; 22:7), faith in Jesus (14:12).

added a speculation about the further course of history, as is the nature of Jewish apocalyptic. "What is to take place" is really future. But individual events of world history to come are not predicted—John rather portrays the characteristic features of all coming history which are disclosed by the victory of Jesus Christ. Thus the Seer is at liberty to adopt traditional schemes and, with the help of various symbolic devices, to set forth this time.

The tension of the End time is resolved primarily by the Parousia of Christ, the final revelation and accomplishment of salvation. The Revelation sees in the coming of Christ the beginning of a new "history," which, by means of the millennial kingdom, the judgment of the world, leads the new Jerusalem to the new Paradise. John describes the End under various aspects and shows thereby that he is not satisfied with the mere laying out of a rigid scheme of eschatological events and that he is aware of the inadequacy of our conceptions. But he accommodates all elements in a total compass and presents the materialization of salvation as a consequence of events whose unfolding lies grounded in the nature of salvation history. That John accordingly represents the consummation of the renewed world as an event in time, as a succession of God's several creative intrusions, is not only related to the fact that we must speak of the coming final future in earthbound images, but also shows that it is only in this temporal context that it can be spoken of at all, since the coming salvation will bring the consummation and fulfillment of promises. However, this activating principle of promise and fulfillment constitutes history.

And finally, it ought to be noted that, for John as for the whole New Testament, salvation does not mean the immortality of the soul, but the bodily resurrection, a re-creation of this, our earthly existence, from both heaven and earth and thus from space and time. And John is perfectly clear about this, that we do not really know the actualities about which we speak, even though we can speak about them only in this way and in no other (cf. 3:12; 19:12, and 1 John 3:2).

IV

The Consummation

1. THE MILLENNIAL KINGDOM

The history of the consummation begins in the Revelation as in the rest of the New Testament with the Parousia (19:11ff.). The succession of events in 19:11ff. depends on traditional patterns, yet in many ways the material is treated quite independently. An inner causal relationship exists between the construction of the consummation's story and the overall historical outlook of the Revelation.

The Revelation clearly depends on the pattern of Ezekiel 37–48, which the following organization shows:

Resurrection of Israel and messianic kingdom (37)—Gog from Magog (38–39)—new temple, portrayal of the new city and country (40–48).

The connection with this pattern makes any attempt to see in Revelation 19:11ff. a recapitulation of the vision series lying before 19:11ff.[1] extremely questionable and testifies to a purely futuristic understanding. Ezekiel's scheme is however not slavishly assumed, but is altered essentially and in various ways. Thus Ezekiel lacks the portrayal of the final judgment and of Paradise; the destruction of Gog is already applied in the Revelation to the image of the destruction of the Antichrist. And other dislocations will yet be shown. This fact must restrain one from interpreting the images of the Revelation simply according to Ezekiel.[2]

---

1 Cf. on the whole problem especially the inclusive, excellent monograph of H. Bietenhard, *Das tausendjährige Reich* (1955).

2 Cf. Kuhn, *TWB* 1:790ff.; Bietenhard, *op. cit.*, pp. 33–37; see also footnote 26 of this chapter.

The millennial kingdom is introduced by the chaining of the dragon "that he should deceive the nations no more" (20:1-3). His power to deceive has remained in him even after his fall from heaven (12:10; cf. Isa. 24:21f.). Thereupon, using words from Daniel 7:9f., thrones are described, "then, that creatures sit upon them who are thus recognized as judges, and finally, just who these judges are."[3] Their installation into office occurs with the resurrection.[4]

Those resurrected are designated with two descriptions and distinguished as two groups: the martyrs and (introduced with *kai hoitines*) all who have withstood the persecution of the beast without having paid with their lives. Thus they together constitute the church of Jesus, including, of course, the ancient people of God whose attachment to Jesus is maintained in 12:1.[5] They now come with Christ to lordship over the old earth for a thousand years.

The number 1000 undoubtedly stems from a world-epoch scheme (the equivalent of a world-week). Moreover, it is completely isolated in the Revelation. Therefore, such speculations ought not be implicitly introduced into the book. We have seen rather that John's numbers, which originally marked out specific spaces of time, have been dissociated from the thought of a definite duration and have become expressions of the quality of a time and its history without reference to its calculable length (cf. 3½ times, 42 months, 1260 days, all as definitions of the End time). Thus also this number 1000 qualifies a critical part of God's action with men. The number does not involve any kind of statement about the duration of the manifestation of Jesus' victory on the old earth. The law of (negative) parallelism which we have seen before plays its role again. The victory of Jesus and his church stands over against the victory of the Antichrist and his followers (ch. 13). And in this connection the imposing dimension of the number of Jesus' victory gets its

---

3 Lohmeyer, *op. cit., ad loc.* The same range of ideas stands behind this image as is evident in 1 Corinthians 6:2f. Cf., for the Jewish interpretation of the Daniel passage, Volz, *op. cit.*, p. 276.

4 *Kai ezēsan*, after Ezekiel 37:10. Even Romans 14:9 uses *ezēsen* of the resurrection of Jesus. The description of the resurrection in 11:11 is likewise dependent on Ezekiel 37. Cf. A. Wikenhauser, "Das Problem des tausendjährigen Reiches in der Joh. Apk.," *RQ* 40 (1932), pp. 18f., and H. Bietenhard, *op. cit.*, pp. 23, 35.

5 Justin also understood the passage this way, *Dial.* 81:4: "Those who believe in our Christ will spend a thousand years in Jerusalem."

meaning in comparison with the 3½ times (and 3½ days) of the Antichrist.

What meaning does the millennium now have in the context of the whole historical view of John? It concerns the unveiling of the reality of the church of Jesus, hidden during the whole of the End time. Of course, the messianic Basileia does not have its beginning here for it has already been realized in the church, but yet not in evidence for unbelievers, the church being bound up in trial and endurance (1:9). Thus the millennial kingdom is the second step, the revelation of this kingdom.[6]

The hiddenness and apparent unreality of the church's existence as the community of messianic salvation, which appears to the world as a pure illusion and empty assertion, cry out for its revelation to the world. The millennium as an obvious messianic kingdom is hence the proof of the divine truthfulness of the word given to the believer and of the testimony of the "true witness," which is "The Word of God" in person (19:13). The Logos-name of Jesus stands in an inner connection with the event of the millennium.

The office of Jesus' community in view of the revelation of its glory can therefore be none other than that held during the whole End time: a priesthood for God and Christ (20:6).

We must answer yet one more question. Many interpreters, sensitive to the peculiar ambiguity of Judaism in the New Testament, have brought together the enigmatic image of the millennium and consideration of Israel's hope.[7] It has been frequently pointed out in this connection that the spatial center of this kingdom would be the earthly Jerusalem. According to Revelation 20:9, the last hosts of the enemy, who are gathered by Gog and Magog after the one thousand years, are of course marched up "over the broad earth" and surround the camp of the saints and the beloved city. However, there is no concrete localizing of the event. The attack on the broad earth is traditional (Ezek. 38:12, 16; Hab. 1:6; Enoch 56:5, etc.). "The beloved city" is an expression parallel to

---

6 See O. Cullmann, "The Kingship of Christ and the Church in the NT," *The Early Church* (1956), p. 113: ". . . the whole Regnum Christi forms a unity, as is already evident from the fact that the phase which precedes the Parousia merely represents a kind of recapitulation of the phase which is to follow it."

7 Cf. H. Bietenhard, *op. cit.*, pp. 90ff.

Zion (after Pss. 78:68; 87:2). Zion, however, is completely divorced from its geographical significance in the Revelation and has become a designation of the Christian church's meaning in salvation's history. "The camp of the saints," which obviously means the same thing, is not to be localized either. We can learn what the camp means from the new texts from Palestine, in which the covenant community is termed "host of saints," or camp.[8]

It may at least briefly be pointed out that John, with his hope for a first resurrection to be followed by still further eschatological acts of God, does not stand alone in the primitive Christian church. Even if the special form of the millennial kingdom, by which John gives expression to his hopes, is lacking in Paul's letters, we still find similar thoughts expressed in 1 Thessalonians 4:13–18 and 1 Corinthians 15:21ff. If I put the two passages side by side, I am aware that very different occasions prompted the writing of these two letters regarding the eschatological hope, and that therefore we do not encounter in the two letters any systematic outline from Paul, but only a clarification of single significant problems. Yet, behind all this a clear overall conception is visible, which Paul suits to his particular situations. And there has not yet come to light any conclusive evidence indicating that Paul had altered the form of his eschatological hopes between the two letters.[9]

In 1 Thessalonians 4:13–18, according to a "word of the Lord," the resurrection of the faithful in the time of Christ's Parousia is anticipated. Those faithful still living at that time will be taken up with the dead when the Parousia occurs.[10] Thus only the church of Jesus has any place in this discussion. What happens with the other people is not said, nor anything of a second resurrection.

---

8 1QM, 1QSa and b, DJD I, DCD; cf. the passages by K. G. Kuhn, *Konkordanz zu den Qumran-Texten* (1960), *s.v. machaneh*.

9 Unhappily, there are people who always scent danger when they admit nonpermanent divergences in any biblical witnesses and they, so hindered, have their clever constructions interfered with.

10 Only the glorified will be given final union with the Lord, 1 Corinthians 15:50, 53. If this union is to happen at the Parousia then the "transfiguration" must be expected only for the believers of the last generation, as Paul brings out in 1 Corinthians 15:51f. (note here the wholly similar definition of the point of time as in 1 Thess. 4). That in 1 Thessalonians 4 only the destiny of the dead is closely described, is grounded in the theme of the section (1 Thess. 4:13!) and it is not justifiable to doubt "whether Paul had the conception of the transfiguration testified to in 1 Corinthians 15:50ff. at the time of 1 Thessalonians" (M. Dibelius, *op. cit., ad loc.*).

But does it not follow from the special place of the church at the Parousia that Paul knows of a special later act for the others in the eschatological event?

This appears to be the actual case in 1 Corinthians 15:23–28.

The text will be discussed more precisely later. In any case, here Paul sees the eschatological event beginning with the resurrection of Jesus Christ, followed later (*epeita*) by the resurrection of the Christian believers (cf. 1 Thess. 4:13ff.). But 1 Corinthians goes well beyond 1 Thessalonians 4, in that here a still later event is proclaimed by a broader temporal concept (*eita*) which expresses a thing temporally later. This, and the fact that between the first two eschatological acts, the resurrection of Christ and the resurrection of the believers, there lies an intermediary time, allows us to assume that the second and third eschatological acts are also thought of as separated by such a longer or shorter period—wholly apart from what must be understood by the *telos* in verse 24. Why 1 Thessalonians 4:17 should have excluded the final drama after the Parousia[11] cannot be determined, although there has been given an answer there only to the special question as to the destiny of the faithful who "sleep" at the Parousia. What happens to the rest of the world is not said, for Paul has no ground for further information on this. That in general only the believers came into consideration because Paul's teaching was that the others would be destroyed,[12] is certainly incorrect, as W. Michaelis has shown.[13] Between the second and third eschatological events is a period of time which must be considered, according to 1 Corinthians 15:24–28, a period in which the *katargein* of the powers occurs, and after whose conclusion the Son then gives the lordship over to the Father.

Thus it appears to be thoroughly possible that Paul here is thinking of the same period which the Revelation describes as the millennium. Hering has, to the contrary, asserted that Paul knew only of a messianic kingdom prior to the Parousia.[14] Certainly we have also encountered the same understanding of the messianic

---

11 J. Hering, "Paul a-t-il enseigné deux résurrections?" *RHPR* (1932), p. 315.
12 Hering, *ibid.*, p. 303.
13 W. Michaelis, *Versöhnung des Alls,* pp. 72–79.
14 Hering, *op. cit.*, pp. 312ff.

kingdom in the Revelation, and we shall see that the millennium, which cannot be marked off from the intermediary time by the idea of the "messianic kingdom," is only the final phase and full revelation of this one messianic kingdom. Paul can also be understood thus. 1 Corinthians 15 certainly does not speak explicitly of this final phase. However, this does not prove in any way its nonexistence in the Pauline eschatological conceptions, and 1 Corinthians 15, as we have seen, in its extremely narrow development of eschatology, allows room in any case for this "mystery."[15] And it may also be pointed out that a wholly similar conception as in Revelation 20:4 perhaps also is present in 1 Corinthians 6:2f., where Paul speaks of the coming judgment of the cosmos at the hands of the faithful.[16]

Paul speaks—as over against Judaism—in a wholly new manner, when he speaks of the resurrection of the faithful.[17] And we nowhere find in Paul any association of the first resurrection with the theme of "Israel."[18]

2. THE FINAL JUDGMENT

After the millennium comes the general world judgment. Who sits on the throne is not expressly identified. It is natural to think of God's throne from Revelation 4:2f., yet it is not to be forgotten that Christ also possesses the eschatological judgmental power (cf. the conclusions of the messages to the churches); he had sat on the throne with God (3:21) and bears the sword of judgment (1:16). It is quite wrong to perceive the second resurrection in the event of world judgment: mankind stands before the throne in

---

15 Cf. also K. L. Schmidt, *Die Polis in Kirche und Welt, Rektoratsprogramm der Universität Basel* (1939), p. 38: "The chiliasm clearly developed in Revelation 20 lies concealed by Paul in 1 Corinthians 15:23–28." So also G. Schrenk, *Die Weissagung über Israel im NT* (1951), p. 71, footnote 63.

16 The cosmos can include in verse 2 not only the angelic powers, as Hering, *op. cit.*, pp. 302f., and *La première epître de S. Paul aux Corinthiens*, pp. 43f., postulates, for the context has to do with their judicial competence over men, and the two statements in verses 2 and 3 do not stand parallel but in connection with a climax: in the second statement it is emphasized that even the angels (as the highest creatures of the cosmos or as the "rulers of this age," 1 Cor. 2:8) will come within the scope of the judgment of the redeemed (cf. W. Foerster, *TWB* 3:892).

17 Cf. Alb. Schweitzer, *op. cit.*, p. 94.

18 The conception of a first resurrection of the dead of the land of Israel in the messianic time emerges in the third century. The righteous buried outside the land will enter into life in Israel by means of subterranean caves. Cf. Strack and Billerbeck, *op. cit.*, III:827–830.

their death condition, as *nekroi* (20:12). The living are already resurrected; their decision has already been sealed by the first resurrection. "He who believes in him is not condemned; he who does not believe is condemned already" (John 3:18). It concerns precisely this crisis. The single decisive measure of this action of judgment is that of belonging to the Lamb (20:15; cf. 13:8). There is an apparent lack of harmony here, with the books of works (20:12) standing near the book of life, which alone possesses decisive meaning (20:15!). However, there is really no such lack of harmony here, any more than there is in the Pauline interpretation of judgment (cf. for instance Rom. 2:5f.; 1 Cor. 3:13ff.). Exactly the same meaning is found in the Revelation as in Paul, that no one is justified by works (Rev. 1:5 *et al.*). But precisely the fact that these sinful works are mentioned gives the unique redemption by the Lamb its "seriousness and profundity." "It is self-evident that the thought of justification without works does away with the thought of a judgment according to works, but in such a way that the latter is included as still valid, not so as to exclude it as a falsehood or error."[19]

Revelation 20:11ff. evidently does not hope that a part of the dead, who thus have not yet taken part in the first resurrection, will be saved from before the lake of fire. Rather, the judgment serves to reveal those who continue in sin without making repentance (2:16; 21:8), who have not sought forgiveness from Christ (22:14f.). The Revelation speaks of the reality of this eschatological judgment in agreement with the whole New Testament: there are sins for which no forgiveness remains "either in this age or in the age to come" (Matt. 12:32 and parallels).

In the Revelation as in the whole New Testament, forgiveness is granted with a view to the coming of the judge and promises protection from the last and highest effect of the divine wrath.[20] Unfor-

---

19 F. Büchsel, *TWB* 3:939. On the change in understanding of the last judgment in more recent theological work, cf. the instructive work of J. P. Martin, *The Last Judgement in Protestant Theology from Orthodoxy to Ritschl* (1963). Cf. footnote 26.

20 Matthew 12:32 says nothing about the finality of the judgmental situation, emphasizing only the inescapability of the penalty which awaits in the age to come. With the help of the aeon concept there is indicated in the New Testament concerning the future punitive situation only its immeasurably long duration, and, by means of *aiōnios,* its eschatological importance (see pp. 31ff.). Cf. W. Michaelis, *op. cit.,* pp. 49ff.

given sin means accordingly nonprotection from the eschatological penalty and points to a condition of hardness of heart which simply cannot be undone before the hour of world judgment (cf. Heb. 10:26f.).[21]

3. THE SECOND DEATH

The judge's judicial sentence now drives the destroyer "Death" and the prince of Hades, along with all men who have been found guilty, into the place of eschatological judgment. Previously, after the victory of the returning Christ, the Antichrist and the false prophet and, immediately before the world judgment, the devil, had been thrown into it (19:20; 20:10). This place of punishment is described as the lake of fire in which God's final wrathful judgment is disclosed.[22] In 20:14 and 21:8, this place is called the second *thanatos*. A traditional idea is no doubt being adopted here.[23] It is conceived here as wholly impersonal and is best translated by "second dying," or, for it involves a special situation of persons, as "a second being dead, second condition of death."[24] Obviously, this expression is intended to suggest a connection with the "first death situation." What binds the two is the thought that they are an expression of an action of divine judgment (cf. III, 4). For the unredeemed, the first death brings an existence in the realm of death, the second death brings an existence in the lake of fire. To restrict the idea of the eschatological existence of death only to men, as Michaelis proposes,[25] is quite inappropriate, for in all the passages where this place of eschatological judgment is spoken of, it is really one and the same thing, a matter of a disaster which, as over against the first situation, is temporally later and sharpened.[26]

These considerations and the related direct statement that this disastrous situation, this "perdition,"[27] means torture "for ever and ever" (20:10), excludes the idea that there might be the alterna-

---

21 Cf. on this especially K. L. Schmidt, "Die Verstockung des Menschen durch Gott," *ThZ* 1 (1945), pp. 1–17.

22 Cf. W. Bousset, *Eschatologie*, p. 279; E. Böklen, *op. cit.*, pp. 119f.

23 Cf. Strack and Billerbeck, *op. cit.*, III:830f.

24 Philippians 1:20 also designates the condition of death by *thanatos*. Cf. R. Bultmann, *TWB* 3:13.

25 Michaelis, *op. cit.*, pp. 107–109, 115.

26 To this explanation cf. my book *Die Zukunft der Welt* (1966).

27 *Apōleia*, Revelation 17:8, 11. Cf. Oepke, *TWB* 1:396.

tives here of "endless torturing" or "final destruction."[28] The wording of 20:10 forbids thinking of a dissolution into nothingness, although the duration of the situation is not concretely limited by the aeon concept, but is recognized only as inconceivably long.

Since the Revelation—as we shall see—knows a suspension of this accursed condition, the importance of this eschatological disaster is to be brought into association with the meaning of salvation history, which the thought of judgment also possesses in the Revelation. God's chastising love is also to be thought of here, which love is permitted to fall into the very abysses of divine condemnation and reprobation in order to lead the reprobate creation to repentance in boundless grace for its salvation and re-creation. The atoning effect of suffering is not in mind here at all. Chastising can only produce a disposition to repentance; that is, a readiness to receive the atonement which the Lamb of God has made.

4. THE SECOND RESURRECTION

It has already been pointed out that the second resurrection, which is not directly mentioned in the Revelation, is nevertheless presumed after 20:6 and should not be sought for in the event of world judgment. Not once is there the slightest hint in the text of this understanding, and furthermore it must not be overlooked that "resurrection" in 20:5f. designates the entry of the redeemed into full possession of eschatological salvation, whereby the number, which suggests a temporal succession, emphasizes the real homogeneity of the two resurrections (as with the first and second conditions of death). The second resurrection—like the first—can accordingly designate only the bestowal of eternal life. Since the first resurrection brings redemption from the first death situation, it is proper to understand the second resurrection as redemption from the second death situation. The idea of the second resurrection, the redemption of those who suffer under God's wrathful eschatological judgment, bears thus in itself the hope for the reconciliation of all men, even of the universe. This hope for the consummation of the whole creation through the grace of the Lamb

---

28 So W. Hadorn, *op. cit.*, p. 202; most commentators agree with him.

is proclaimed in the worship, so full of promise, of the representatives of the creation, the four living creatures and twenty-four elders of chapters 4–5. Their worship has also an extremely comforting sound, for it is the confession out of the tortured mouths of those who have endured the blows of the Antichrist and his worshipers (15:4): that some day "all nations shall come and worship" the Lord. How this thought broadens in effect in the Revelation, we have yet to see.

A wholly similar conception appears to be present in Luke 14:14, where a "resurrection of the just" is spoken of, which presumes a temporally later, general resurrection, not to be identified with appearing before the judgment.[29]

The same understanding of the resurrection hope as in the Revelation lies behind 1 Corinthians 15. Here, the resurrection hope is grounded on the "life-giving spirit," Jesus Christ (1 Cor. 15:45). Paul gives a more precise exposition of this hope in verses 21-28. He starts from the inescapable fate of death for all men, which is occasioned by the real association of all men with the sinful nature of Adam, the ancestor of mankind. And now in the programmatic sentences of 15:21f. there is exhibited the meaning of salvation history, grounded as it is in the resurrection of Christ himself, in regard to its beginning and its goal, and the final consequences of Christ's act of salvation are disclosed. "For as in Adam all die, so also in Christ shall all be made alive." The two parts of the sentence stand parallel, and so we have no reason at all in the second part to limit the "all" in the least degree, for the first "all," which speaks of bodily death, cannot be limited

---

29 For, even in the synoptic Gospels, John, and Acts, "resurrection" indicates entry into full salvation (cf. for instance Matt. 22:28–32 and parallels; Acts 17:18; John 11:25). Even Hebrews 6:2 presents no occasion to understand the resurrection, which constitutes a contrast to the judgment, as other than an entering into full salvation (as the "rising to a better life," Heb. 11:35). And it stands this way in Paul as well (cf. Rom. 6:5; Phil. 3:11; 2 Tim. 2:18). Only in John 5:28f. is there an *anastasis* to life and to judgment spoken of, and in Acts 24:15, a resurrection of the just and unjust, and thus a simultaneous general resurrection. But in John 5 there is an idea like that of "coming forth out of the grave," which means hence only "standing up"—out of the grave, from the sleep of death, or out of the realm of death (cf. *anastasis* without reference to the resurrection of the dead, Luke 2:34). And Acts 24:15 is best understood this way also. Thus there is here as in Revelation 20:12f. the belief that the dead arise and are gathered for judgment, which will bring entry into "life" or into condemnation. A similar idea is found in Syriac Baruch 50:1–51:10: first of all, the dead will appear before God in the same form "as they had received on earth," and after the judgment their "appearance will change."

either. Verse 22 intends not only "to show that the Christians may hope for their resurrection,"[30] as the broadly conceived discussion of salvation history in the following verses shows. And precisely here must Paul's meaning be further ascertained, since with his unprecedented affirmation the whole question of the future plan of salvation is called forth. The "being made alive" in 15:22 can thereby only be interpreted as an entry into the full possession of salvation with a spiritual corporeality,[31] for 15:22 stands fully parallel to 15:21, where in place of the verbs "die" and "be made alive" the nouns "death" and "resurrection" are inserted. In 15:35f., where the "how" of the spiritual resurrection reality is spoken of, Paul likewise uses "make alive" synonymously with the bestowal of the resurrection body (cf. the same use of the idea in Rom. 4:17 and 8:11) and Christ, who procures the resurrection, is called in 15:45 "life-giving spirit."

The resurrection of mankind is now accomplished through three eschatological events. It begins with the resurrection of Christ, is carried on with the resurrection of Christian believers at the Parousia, and reaches its consummation at the "End." That *to telos* cannot mean "remnant," J. Hering has unequivocally demonstrated.[32] For an explanation of the word it is to be observed that it corresponds with the "first fruits" idea of 1 Corinthians 15:23. *Aparchē* signifies Christ's resurrection as a promise for the whole. This whole is evidently to be sought in the "all." Thus the promise which is given in the resurrection of Jesus the first fruits comes to a first fulfillment in the resurrection of the believers and reaches its "End" in a third event. And that can only mean, according to 15:22f., that all the rest of mankind comes to the resurrection, so that there is fulfilled: *houtōs kai en tō Christō pantes zōopoiēthēsontai*. The statement that each man will be resurrected in his appointed *tagma* appears to relate to these three events. That at least three *tagmata* are presumed is Hering's thought also, except that he would interpret them according to 1 Thessalonians 4:16ff.,

---

30 W. G. Kümmel, on Corinthians I and II, in *Hdb. L.* (1949), p. 193; cf. p. 169; Bietenhard, *op. cit.*, pp. 56ff.

31 This must be maintained against Michaelis, *op. cit.*, p. 181, footnote 190.

32 Hering, *RHPR* (1932), pp. 304f.

which does not provide any basis for them. Clearly, it is much more realistic to seek the third resurrection group in the *telos* event.

This does not mean a "narrowing of the Pauline statement," as Michaelis writes,[33] when Hering, in his commentary on 15:22, points to the fact that "in Christ" must be understood precisely as being part of the body of Christ. But Hering draws false conclusions from this. It is quite so that for Paul the formation of the body of the Lord is not yet concluded with the time of the earthly existence of the church, but that the body of Christ increases yet further after the Parousia until it has taken all into itself: "For from him and through him and to him are all things" (Rom. 11:36, Col. 1:16). Paul maintains with this formulation that there is a resurrection only "in Christ." Now, of course, all are not yet in Christ, nor even at the time of the Parousia, but yet this condition will be entered into by all, so that the whole of mankind will become the "body of Christ." Not till then is the atoning work of Christ accomplished and his lordship given over to the Father.

According to 15:24-26, the spiritual powers as well enter into the totality of men. Even they shall have a portion in God's glory when the "End" is reached. What happens to them is expressed with *katargein*. What is this intended to mean?[34] The spiritual powers are, according to 15:25, enemies of Christ, for Psalm 110:1 (cf. Ps. 8:6) is applied to them. Even death is one of them (15:26).[35] The *katargein* of these powers consists in their being put under Christ's feet, thus fully conquered. This victory of Christ is interpreted in 15:27 as *hypotassein* of the powers. The significance of this word becomes quite clear in the following verse, for 15:28 means that even the Son, when all things have been subjected to him, is himself "subjected." His "subjection" consists in his giving over, as a Son, his previously exercised lordship to the Father (15:24). *Katargein* is thus best translated as "deprive of power": the spiritual powers are deprived of their arrogated power against

---

33 Michaelis, *op. cit.*, p. 85.

34 Cf. the discussion by Cullmann, *op. cit.*, p. 114, and K. Barth, "Rechtfertigung und Recht," *ThSt* 14 (1938), pp. 16f.

35 It will not do to term death, which stands in a series with the other enemies as a personified power, "merely a final end, not a person in the sense of those powers," as Michaelis desires to do, *op. cit.*, p. 168, footnote 71.

God. This means, however: they are brought back to their proper creaturely order by Christ, so that God can be "all things" to them also (15:28; cf. Phil. 2:9f.). The goal of the whole plan of salvation thus also consists in 1 Corinthians 15 in the atonement and resumption of all creation into God's consummated kingdom.

5. THE NEW JERUSALEM

After the world judgment, there now begins the second resurrection and the re-creation of the world. We shall see that there is involved not simply a single event, but a newly beginning consummation history.

The following scenes hence are solemnly contrasted with all that has existed hitherto by a long introduction, 21:1-8. Against all efforts to engage in source analyses and textual emendations in chapters 21–22, there must be observed an indissoluble connection between 21:1-8 and the concluding portion of the book. 21:1-8 is a prologue which introduces this final part. Here, as there, are three parts to be clearly discerned: 21:1-4 speaks of a new Jerusalem which is then portrayed in 21:9-27; 21:5 refers to the scene in 22:1-5, which is clearly contrasted with what precedes it; 21:6-8 closes with an exhortation which is more richly developed in 22:6-21.

As was earlier suggested, the new Jerusalem can only be understood as the fulfillment of the special eschatological hope for the chosen people of Israel. As in Matthew 19:28, the special hope of Israel is first expected here at the "palingenesis," at the re-creation of the world.[36] In the new Jerusalem the history of Israel, which is carried forward in the Jewish-Christian remnant and the whole Christian church until the new Jerusalem, comes to its goal.

The relationship with the scheme of Ezekiel 37 points to this interpretation of the new Jerusalem in Revelation 21. We have seen

---

36 Luke 22:30 puts "my kingdom" for this. Any special reference or limitation of the "palingenesis" to Israel is lacking in the text. It is questionable whether there is any mention of a judicial or ruling office of the apostle here (cf. G. Schrenk, *op. cit.*, pp. 17ff.), but in any case Jesus considers the new aeon to begin with a special, new action toward the old Covenant people. The Revelation stands—like Matthew 19:28—in a line of tradition with Isaiah 65:17ff.: a hope for Israel aimed primarily toward a "new earth."

that the picture of the messianic kingdom in Ezekiel 37 was transferred to the time of the church and especially so in the case of the kingdom's glorification in the millennium. According to its universal view, the Revelation splices in the final judgment and then carries Ezekiel's scheme further. In Ezekiel, the new Jerusalem with its temple and the whole land follows the portrayal of Gog and his destruction as a fulfillment of the national hope of Israel (Ezek. 40–48). The Seer has thus connected Israel's promises with this city. It bears the honored name "the holy city," "the holy city Jerusalem" (21:2, 10). In it is fulfilled the promise which could not be fulfilled in the earthly Jerusalem. It is no longer the earthly Jerusalem which will be glorified and renewed, for that earthly city had lost its significance for salvation since it crucified its Lord. The new Jerusalem is primarily expected for the renewed world, it comes down from heaven as God's new creation of grace. This heavenly city bears the signs of God's faithfulness to his word which he has given to his people: its gates bear the names of the twelve tribes of the sons of Israel, as Ezekiel promises (Ezek. 48:30ff.; Rev. 21:12). "God is not man, that he should lie . . . Has he said, and will he not do it? Or has he spoken, and will he not fulfil it?" (Num. 23:19).[37]

Besides the connection with Ezekiel the association with Isaiah 60 is also significant, and we must clarify it a bit. Following Isaiah 60 it is said that the city will have no need of sun or moon, for the Lord himself will be its light, with the Lamb, that the nations will walk in its light and the kings of the earth will bring their glory into it, that its gates will not be shut day and night. The vision of the new Jerusalem distinctly and deliberately connects Isaiah 60 with the words spoken at the beginning, in the letter to the church at Philadelphia. That the Seer has consciously made this connection shows that he ties that church's letter to the promise of the new Jerusalem: "I will write on [the conqueror] the name of my God, and the name of the city of my God, the New Jerusalem which comes down from my God out of heaven" (3:12). Of the Jews, however, he writes in the same letter: "Behold, I will make

---

37 Cf. especially K. L. Schmidt, *op. cit.*, pp. 25ff.; *Aus der Johannes-Apokalypse* (1944), pp. 52ff.; also footnote 26.

those of the synagogue of Satan who say that they are Jews and are not, but lie—behold, I will make them come and bow down before your feet, and learn that I have loved you" (3:9). The meaning of Isaiah 60:14 is the same: "The sons of those who oppressed you shall come bending low to you; and all who despised you shall bow down at your feet; they shall call you the City of the LORD, the Zion of the Holy One of Israel." But this means a remarkable inversion in the Revelation: the church is now oppressed, and that at the hands of the unbelieving Jews, and these— like the heathen in Isaiah 60—enter into the community of the Lord. The words of the Revelation thus do not promise a special fruitfulness of the mission to the Jews in Philadelphia, but express a highly inclusive eschatological promise: in the New Jerusalem the yet unbelieving Jews will some day be gathered! And again we stand very near the Pauline expectation, "a hardening has come upon part of Israel, until the full number of the Gentiles come in, and so all Israel will be saved" (Rom. 11:25f.).[38]

That "all Israel" refers to Israel according to the flesh appears to me to be made quite certain by K. L. Schmidt's study of Romans 9–11.[39] The use of the honored name "Israel" in verse 25 for the "hard of heart" and thus the unbelievers, as well as the emphasizing of Israel's prerogatives in Romans 1:16 and 2:9f., and above all the basing of the entire attitude in Romans 9–11 on the faithfulness of God to Israel in the flesh and the promises made to them (9:3-5; 11:28), which have not been abrogated by their unfaithfulness (3:3f.; 11:29), the emphasizing of the enduring significance of Israel by Paul's adherence to membership in Israel in the flesh (2 Cor. 11:22; Phil. 3:5), and also the whole discussion about the promissory character of Israel's remnant (Rom. 11:1-24)—these things together guarantee the interpretation that by "all Israel" the totality of Israel in the flesh is meant. Paul's universalism—as becomes clearly evident in 1 Corinthians 15 (cf. Sect. 4) and as his

---

38 Cf. K. L. Schmidt, "Die Judenfrage im Lichte der Kapitel 9–11 des Römerbriefes," *ThSt* 13 (1943); G. Schrenk, *Der göttliche Sinn in Israels Geschick* (1943); W. Vischer, "Der neue Staat Israel und der Wille Gottes," *ThZ* 9 (1953), pp. 29ff.

39 K. L. Schmidt, *op. cit.*, p. 68. Here is an elaboration of the whole discussion.

phrase moreover indicates[40]—as well as the whole Pauline historical-theological view of the consequence of the Christ event of the past for all times, compels us to think in Romans 11:26 not only of the Jews of the last generation but also of those dead in unbelief. "All Israel" is inclusive in the spatial as well as the temporal sense.

In Romans 11:15, this salvation is called *proslēmpsis,* "acceptance." It has a prominent place in the history of God with the world as a sign of promise which points with unprecedented breadth to the action of the divine grace. Its effect here is the *apobolē,* as over against the partial condemnation (11:25), which has led to the salvation of the full number of Gentiles. In what does the intensified effect of the acceptance of all Israel consist? It will bring "life out of the dead"! It is generally understood so that by it the whole eschatological event is caused and the resurrection of the dead, the first resurrection in particular, is begun.[41] Romans 11:15 gives however still more concrete information. The verse cannot be torn away from its connection with the whole of the eleventh chapter. In Romans 11 there stands above all in the range of ideas under discussion, the narrowing and widening of the action of divine salvation (cf. the catchwords *leimma,* 11:5; *aparchē,* 11:16; *plērōma, meros,* 11:26; *pas, pantes,* 11:26, 32, 36). Thus also in 11:15 there is in mind not only an intensive exaltation to glory by the resurrection of the faithful, but also the broad extension of the powers of the resurrection over the full number of the Gentiles to a yet greater number, thus to the totality of the dead. With the salvation of all Israel, an avenue is opened to eternal life for all men.

40 Cf. Romans 5:18; 11:32, 36; 2 Corinthians 5:19; Philippians 2:10; 1 Timothy 2:4; 4:10; Colossians 1:20; Ephesians 1:10. G. Schrenk, *Die Weissagung über Israel im NT,* p. 35, does not want to take "all Israel" in the full meaning of the phrase. This does not seem justified to me in this passage, for "all Israel" is emphasized as over against the "remnant" of Israel of the intermediary time. Hence the formalized usage in 1 Samuel 25:1; 1 Kings 12:1; 2 Chronicles 12:1; Acts 13:24, to which G. Schrenk appeals, says nothing at all for our passage.

41 Bietenhard, *op. cit.,* pp. 106f. All applications to a metaphorical understanding of the passage are properly declined by Zahn, *Der Römerbrief, Kommentar zum NT,* Vol. VI (1910), pp. 511f.; cf. also G. Schrenk, *op. cit.,* p. 68, footnote 41. That in Romans 11:15 the conversion of the Jews might be interpreted as the condition for the Parousia and the first resurrection has no support in the text and, moreover, none in the Pauline letters. Paul does not directly mention the place of the readmission of Israel in the eschatological drama.

Thus John, in the twenty-first chapter of his book, views the theological solution of the Jewish question as does Paul, not in the range of historical possibilities in the old aeon, but solely in the perspective of the eschatological consummation beyond this history.

To this interpretation of the new Jerusalem there correspond fully all the details of the scene in chapter 21, which is seen wholly in Old Testament colors. Thus the gates of the city bear the names of the twelve tribes (cf. Ezek. 48:30ff.), which are supplemented by the names of the twelve apostles of the Lamb, and which, on the basis of the pardoning of Israel, point to the act of redemption by the Lamb (proclaimed by the apostles).[42]

The wall "constitutes the city."[43] It has however yet another special function here. It is not thought of as a defensive rampart, for its height is unimportant and its gates always stand open. It has much more of the function of a religious delimiting. It makes visible the fact that at the time of the new Jerusalem there still exists a "within and without" (21:8, 27; 22:15). Obviously, the conception is still in effect here that during the time of the new Jerusalem the lake of fire continues to exist (cf. its duration in 20:10). In this way may be explained the apparent discrepancy between 21:1 and 21:24-27, to which Lohmeyer has pointed. He says that in 21:24-27 "the permanence of the first earth and with it its kings and peoples, its horror and falsehood, are clearly presumed."[44] However, one could make a wreckage of any proper understanding of this if he should assume, on the ground of this apparent discrepancy, that this vision "stands independently among the great major apocalyptic sections" and is not to be classified "in the train of apocalyptic events of 4:1–21:5."[45] This "within and without" while the new Jerusalem still endures is rather to be explained—in line with the whole conception—in this way: the outside can only signify the lake of fire, since the old world has quite perished. All Israel, meaning

---

42 In the image of the *themelioi* the apostolic mission-consciousness finds its expression (as in Eph. 2:20; Matt. 16:18). Cf. O. Cullmann, *Peter* (1962), pp. 220ff.

43 Lohmeyer, *op. cit., ad loc.*

44 *Ibid., ad loc.*

45 *Ibid.*, p. 166. Cf. also Paul Gaechter, *TS* 10 (1949), pp. 492ff. He solves the question by source criticism, postulating two settings of the new Jerusalem, one on earth, the other in heaven. Both belong to the same period of time. The editor is presumed to have been unable to keep the two separated.

those who still remain as unbelievers among the Israelites, will be rescued out of the lake of fire. And it is also indicated by the standing open of the city's gates that during the time of the new Jerusalem rescue is also possible for the Gentiles: the peoples and their leaders will bring their glory in through the gates (21:24f.; cf. Isa. 60:3, 5). Among this renewed people of God there is no longer any need for a temple as a sign of the presence of God, for Israel has now attained with all the faithful the longed-for full fellowship with God (21:22).

6. THE CONSUMMATED WORLD

This eschatological action of God with and toward Israel occurs with an eye toward the whole of humanity. In his last vision, the Seer sees how, right at the End, the city of God is extended to Paradise, so that there is no more *exō,* no existence apart from God: *kai pan katathema ouk estai eti* (22:3).[46] With this there comes to fulfillment the historical destiny which Israel so often had failed at, that of being the mediator of the Covenant and the promising sign of hope for all nations. And therein the Revelation agrees with the Scriptures, above all with the often cited book of Isaiah, which, in 49:6, sings of God's Servant: "It is too light a thing that you should be my servant to raise up the tribes of Jacob and to restore the preserved of Israel; I will give you as a light to the nations, that my salvation may reach to the end of the earth."

The Revelation adheres to the separation of the new Jerusalem from Paradise, this in accord with a part of Jewish apocalyptic,[47] and inserts the imagery into its great framework of consummated history. In this it goes beyond the scheme of Ezekiel, as it did with the image of the final judgment. The new action of God's surpassing grace is proclaimed in the introduction to the last image in 21:5: "Behold, I make *all things* new." This universal statement allows no other interpretation than that the redemption of men and

---

46 On the river of Paradise cf. Genesis 2:10; Ezekiel 47:8ff.; Psalm 46:4; Slavonic Enoch 8:5. On the tree of life cf. Ezekiel 47:12; Genesis 2:9; Slavonic Enoch 8; Ethiopian Enoch 25:4–6.

47 "The Paradise passages as a whole [in the Jewish literature] do not treat of the national hope," but of the universal hope for mankind (Volz, *op. cit.,* pp. 413–418; cf. H. Gunkel, *op. cit.,* pp. 35ff.; W. Bousset, *Die Religion des Judentums,* pp. 282ff.).

powers suffering in the lake of fire is in mind here. Revelation 22:3 thus stands in the closest proximity to the Pauline hope found in 1 Corinthians 15.[48] Thus the whole historical-theological view of our Seer joins in the hope for a reconciliation of the universe. Not only does the exegesis of particular passages point to this, but it is genuinely anchored in the Christian faith of the Apocalyptist. Tendencies toward such a hope are also to be found in Judaism.[49] "There is, however, no clear teaching of the restoration in Judaism."[50] But the Christian view of history, which knows God's faithfulness to all men, to his whole creation, to be anchored in God's overflowing love and grace as revealed in Jesus Christ's redemptive act, has made it possible to have a glimpse into this final secret of salvation's history (Rom. 11:33ff.). And in the Revelation this final creative act of consummated history is bound to the redemptive act of Jesus, who is enthroned with God in Paradise as mankind's atoning Lamb.

---

48 It does not follow from the statement in 21:4, that death shall be no more, that death as a personified power would be destroyed, for the nonpersonified conception of "dying" is involved here (cf. III, 4). This is not taken very seriously by Michaelis, *op. cit.,* p. 115, when he puts 21:4 in association with 20:14 and believes that a line concerning the fate of death "goes out from 20:14 and finds in 21:4 its continuation and, at the same time, its end." Death is redeemed from being a fatal angelic power at enmity with God and made good and peaceful. Cf. p. 123. It is to be noted, over against all the speculative teachings about the restoration, that Paul, as well as John, maintains the complete seriousness of the coming judgment, but also the greater force of Jesus' redemptive victory.

49 Thus Sibylline Oracles 4:44 (in various manuscripts) counts on a recognition of sin and of God in perdition. In Babylonian Rosh Hashanah 16b, 17a, according to the school of Shammai the ordinary sinners will be saved. The Hillelites discriminate more closely. Eduyoth 2:10 has the final judgment on Gog and Magog lasting only twelve months. Whether the suspension of the judgmental situation brings "pardon for the godless or dissolution into nothingness" is quite uncertain (cf. Volz, *op. cit.,* p. 326).

50 *Ibid.,* p. 327. Cf. Strack and Billerbeck, *op. cit.,* IV:1017–1095.

INDEX OF SCRIPTURES

OLD TESTAMENT

JUDAISM

NEW TESTAMENT

INDEX OF NAMES

The full title and date of each work will be found in the place where it is first cited.

TIME AND HISTORY
A Study on the Revelation
By Mathias Rissi

Discovering the meaning of time and history in the book of Revelation is essential to understanding John's purpose and message. Dr. Rissi's theological study on this subject is widely considered one of the most significant books on the Revelation. It is here available for the first time in English.

"What is now and what will be hereafter" are viewed by Dr. Rissi in the perspective of God's eternal purpose for man's salvation. Time and history are interpreted in light of the death and resurrection of Jesus Christ.

This christological approach to Revelation avoids views that tend toward either the fantastic or the irrelevant, and shows how John's message is vitally important for our time. The uniform concept of God's working throughout history offers solutions to many difficult chapters and problems of the book of Revelation.

Dr. Rissi develops his discussion of time and history by detailed examination of the book of Revelation. After explaining the literary structure and its importance for exegesis, he deals with the meaning of time, the end time, and the consummation.

The meaning of time is clarified as Dr. Rissi explains the terminology and arrangement of Revelation and shows the importance of the Lord of time. He analyzes the end time (the time of Christ, the Antichrist, and the church) as it relates to the problems of